DECLINE OF THE GLOBAL VILLAGE:

How Specialization is Changing the Mass Media

Ravi Mehra, *Editor*
Valerie Kressner, *Associate Editor*
GENERAL HALL, INC.
Publishers
23–45 Corporal Kennedy Street
Bayside, New York 11360

Decline
Of The
Global Village

How Specialization is Changing the Mass Media

JAMES E. GRUNIG
Associate Professor
College of Journalism
University of Maryland
College Park, Maryland

GENERAL HALL, INC.
Publishers
23–45 Corporal Kennedy Street
Bayside, New York 11360

DECLINE OF THE GLOBAL VILLAGE:
How Specialization is Changing the Mass Media

Library of Congress Catalog Card Number: 76—9295
Manufactured in the United States of America

Design by   Leota Lamb

Preface

I first became interested in specialized communication as a high school senior in a rural community in Iowa. At that time the United States faced a "farm problem" that today seems strangely out of date. Farm prices were low, and farm incomes equally low. I decided then to go into journalism so that I could communicate information about the economic problems involved and the technological solutions then proposed.

Perhaps I was an unusual journalist. Journalists usually are generalists; I wanted to be a journalist specializing in economics and science. If the thesis of this book is correct, the profession and I may have moved closer together. That thesis is that society is fragmenting into specialized interests, that media are adapting to those interests or new media are being developed to meet those interests, and that the professional communicator will become more specialized in the future in order to meet the demand for specialized information.

The theme of specialization in the media of the future was examined by nine distinguished lecturers during the Sixth Annual Baltimore Sun Lecture Series held at the University of Maryland in April 1974. The series is made possible by a gift from the A. S. Abell Foundation and is sponsored jointly by the College of Journalism and the Baltimore Sunpapers. Those nine lectures provide the core of this book. They include the chapters by Clay T. Whitehead, Ronald P. Kriss, Victor Cohn, David Finn, Jack Lyle, Jonathan Ward, Philip Meyer, Martin Jones, and Jack M. Nilles.

The book contents have been expanded considerably beyond these nine lectures, however, both to provide research evidence to support the specialization thesis and to expose the reader to the views of additional experts in the field of communication. Included in this book are chapters by distinguished professional journalists, communication researchers, and other social scientists.

I have titled the first chapter *Turning McLuhan on His Head* because I wanted to call the reader's attention to the fact that this book is a departure from the conventional wisdom that I think is typified by Marshall McLuhan and other "mass" communication theorists. The mass in communication may once have existed, but if it exists today or in the future it will be because of the economic and institutional interests of the media and not because of the demands of audiences.

Thanks are due to the many people who helped plan the original lecture series and who contributed to the production of this book. Ray E. Hiebert and Lee M. Brown served with me as members of the Distinguished Lectures Committee. Vickie Beard typed the transcripts and edited versions of the lectures. My wife, Jay, and sons, Andy, John, and Neil provided the encouragement needed to complete a project of this nature.

ABOUT THE AUTHORS

James E. Grunig is a communications theorist and researcher with a specialized interest in the economics of the media, science writing, organizational communication and the relationship between communications, economic development and poverty. He holds a B. S. degree from Iowa State University and M. S. and Ph. D. degrees from the University of Wisconsin. He has worked professionally as a science writer and public relations specialist. He is currently associate professor in the College of Journalism, University of Maryland.

Donald E. Skiff is now a technical writer with ReproArt Service in Cincinnati and **J. Paul Yarbrough** is associate professor of journalism and mass communications at Iowa State University. Chapter 2 is abstracted from "Television and Cultural Change," a Master's thesis written by Skiff at Iowa State University in 1970. The thesis resulted from a long—term research project conducted by Yarbrough.

Clay T. Whitehead was director of the Office of Tele—communications Policy in the White House from 1970 to 1974. He was a special assistant to President Nixon from January 1969 until July 1970. Before joining the White House staff, he worked with the Rand Corporation where he helped plan and organize a policy research program for health services and other areas of national policy. Since leaving the the White House, Dr. Whitehead has been working as a con—sultant and writing a book on television and public policy.

Ronald P. Kriss is a senior editor of *Time* magazine and was formerly executive editor of *Saturday Review*. He is a graduate of Harvard University and the Columbia School of Journalism. At the Columbia School of Journalism, he was also the Pulitzer Traveling Scholar. Before joining Time he served two years in Japan as a reporter for the United Press International.

Gary Gumpert is professor of communication arts and sciences at Queens College of the City University of New York. While a Ph. D. candidate at Wayne State University, he served as a producer–director of WTVS–TV.

Richard Maisel is director of graduate studies in the Department of Sociology, New York University, and Fellow of the Laboratory of Community Psychiatry of the Harvard Medical School.

David Finn is chairman of the board and co–founder of Ruder & Finn, Inc., one of the largest public relations firms in the world. Ruder & Finn developed from a two–man operation in 1948 to a firm which now has a staff of 300 people and offices in New York, Toronto, London, Paris, Tokyo, Melbourne, and major cities in the United States. He is the author of *The Corporate Oligarch* and *Public Relations and Management*.

Jack Lyle is director of communication research for the Corporation for Public Broadcasting. He was formerly professor of journalism at UCLA. Lyle has conducted research on educational utilization of mass media, communication problems in urban areas, and children and the mass media. He was one of the researchers working under the Surgeon General's Scientific Advisory Committee on Television and

iv

Social Behavior. He is author of *The News in Megalopolis* and co—author of *Television in the Lives of Our Children* and *The People Look at Educational Television*.

Martin V. Jones is a futurist who has spent the last five years measuring the quality of life and assessing the impact of new technologies on society and individual well—being. Formerly with the MITRE Corporation, he is now director of the Impact Assessment Institute of Bethseda, Maryland. He holds a Ph. D. in economics and business administration from the University of Chicago.

Jack M. Nilles is director of interdisciplinary program development at the University of Southern California. Currently, he is managing an interdisciplinary research program on the telecommunications/transportation tradeoff, which is sponsored by the National Science Foundation. The program is carried out by the Center for Futures Research in the Graduate School of Business Administration at USC under Dr. Paul Gray, in the School of Engineering under Dr. Frederick Carlson, and in the Annenberg School of Communication under Dr. Gerhard Hanneman. Mr. Nilles also has 18 years of military and industrial experience in the areas of transportation, resource management, communications, law enforcement and medical engineering.

Maxwell E. McCombs is a John Ben Snow professor of newspaper research in the School of Public Communications, Syracuse University. He was formerly on the journalism faculty at the University of North Carolina. In addition to the economics of the media, his research interests include political communication and communication theory.

Natan Katzman is research consultant and project

director for the Corporation for Public Broadcasting.

Monroe E. Price is professor of law at the University of California at Los Angeles and is associated with UCLA's communication law program.

Philip Meyer is a leader in the use of social science techniques in reporting. He is the author of *Precision Journalism,* a book explaining how reporters can use these techniques. Meyer is a member of the Washington Bureau of Knight Newspapers, Inc. He was a Nieman fellow at Harvard University in 1966–67, during which time he studied social science techniques and their application to journalism. He was a member of the Detroit *Free Press* team which won a Pulitzer Prize for general assignment reporting in 1968.

Victor Cohn is science and medical reporter and formerly science editor of the *Washington Post.* He was science editor of the Minneapolis *Tribune* from 1946 until he joined the *Post* in 1968. He is the only three–time winner of the Delta Chi, the distinguished service award for general news reporting, a two–time winner of the Westinghouse prize for science reporting awarded by the American Association for the Advancement of Science, and the first winner of the science and society award (for coverage of sickle cell anemia) awarded by the National Association of Science Writers.

Sharon M. Friedman is assistant professor of journalism at Lehigh University and formerly a science writer and information officer for the U. S. International Biological Program.

Jonathan Ward is executive producer, special events with CBS News. Before assuming that position, he "covered the future" for his *Future File,* a series of short reports heard five times weekly on CBS Radio. Ward has conducted over 500 interviews with scientists, scholars, and futurists in an attempt to assess the problems and possibilities of tomorrow. He has won four Chicago Emmy Awards for television writing and directing and a variety of wire service awards for investigative reporting.

Francis Pollock is editor of *Media & Consumer,* P. O. Box 850, Norwalk, Conn. 06852.

Acknowledgements

Grateful acknowledgement is given to the editors and authors for permission to use the following copyrighted articles: Chapter 2 originally appeared as part of "Television and Social Change," Unpublished M.S. Thesis, Iowa State University, Ames, 1970; Chapter 5 appeared in *Journal of Communication* 20 (1970): 280–290; Chapter 6 appeared *Public Opinion Quarterly* 37 (1973): 280–290; Chapter 11 appeared in *Mass Media on the Marketplace, Journalism Monographs* No. 24, August 1972, pp. 38–63; Chapter 12 appeared in *Journal of Communication* 24 (Autumn 1974): 47–58; Chapter 13 appeared in *Journal of Communication* 24 (Summer 1974): 71–76; Chapters 16 and 19 appeared in *Science and the Newspaper,* an occasional paper on science and the media published by the American Association for the Advancement of Science, 1974; Chapter 18 appeared in *Columbia Journalism Review (March/April* 1974): 22–25.

This book is partly the result of the "Baltimore Sun Distinguished Lecture Series," a project of the College of Journalism, University of Maryland. The lectures that are contained in this book were made possible by a grant from the A. S. Abell Company Foundation and the Baltimore Sun—papers.

Special gratitude is due to Mr. William F. Schmick, Jr., President of A. S. Abell Company Foundation; Mr. Perry J. Bolton, Assistant to the President of the Foundation; and Mr. Philip S. Heisler, Managing Editor of the Baltimore Evening Sun, who were instrumental in getting the Lecture Series started.

The purpose of the Lecture Series and its subsequent bbok publication is to provide a forum for the expression of ideas by distinguished journalists, scholars of journalism and others, and to provide a continuing medium of education and exchange between the College of Journalism, its students and alumni, and the journalism profession.

viii

Contents

x

PART I. FROM MASS TO SPECIALIZED COMMUNICATION

Mass and media, mass and communication are word combinations which fit together naturally——almost tautologically——in the popular mind. Contemporary society, it is generally believed, is a mass society either created by or served by mass media. The articles in Part I challenge this conventional wisdom. Not only do these chapters indicate that the future of the media is specialization, but they present a strong case that the media of the future are already upon us.

Part I begins with an original essay by the editor which sets the theme for the rest of the book by challenging McLuhan's popular notion that the medium is the message. Instead, the essay presents a theory of media use and demand for the media which states that people use media either for help in solving problems or for diversion, and that which media they use depends upon the relevance of the content to their needs or tastes.

Because American society is becoming a post—industrial, service and information—oriented system, interests are

1

becoming more specialized and concurrently the demand for information and media appears also to be becoming increasingly specialized.

The chapter by Skiff and Yarbrough present evidence to support the "turning of McLuhan on his head." Skiff and Yarbrough review McLuhan's theory and then present evidence that his theory is inadequate. Finally, Whitehead and Kriss attempt to predict the future of communication in general and of the media in particular.

TURNING McLUHAN ON HIS HEAD

James E. Grunig

The past went that—a—way. When faced with a totally new situation, we tend always to attach ourselves to the objects, to the flavor of the most recent past. We look at the present through a rear—view mirror. We march backwards into the future. Suburbia lives imaginatively in Bonanza—land. (Marshall McLuhan[1])

Marshall McLuhan's rear—view mirror dictum recognizes a condition that perhaps afflicts all human beings. Because we have experienced only the past, seldom do we recognize the present, or anticipate the future. The condition is so universal, in fact, that it now seems to have afflicted McLuhan himself. Because America once was a mass society characterized by mass media and mass culture, McLuhan and his millions of disciples have failed to recognize that we now are becoming a specialized, fragmented society accompanied by an increasingly specialized media system.

For many years, sociologists characterized America as a mass society, which consisted of an amorphous blob of people with little in common other than that their eye—

balls were glued to a television set or a newspaper at the same time. Such a society, it was believed, could easily be manipulated through the media by a power elite or by some sort of military—industrial complex. Thus, mass so— ciety critics have often blamed the media for the decline of family, community, and other desirable group associations.

However, the majority of communication theorists have rejected the notion that the media reach and manipulate isolated defenseless individuals ever since Katz and Lazarsfeld "discovered people" in their voting studies of the 1940's.[2] Their research made it clear that people live and work in social groups and that those social re— lationships determine how people use the media, rather than the other way around. People use the media because the media provide information which has some social utility ——i.e., information which people can share and discuss with others.[3]

Just as the tide was sweeping out on the mass society hypothesis, McLuhan came along to embrace it in an en— tirely new way. In contrast to the sociologists, McLuhan viewed the mass society created by television as an im— provement. Millions of individuals now were becoming totally involved with one another:

In tribal societies we are told that it is a familiar reaction, when some hideous event occurs, for some people to say, "How horrible it must be to feel like that," instead of blaming somebody for having done something horrible. This feeling is an aspect of the new mass culture we are moving into——a world of total involvement in which every— body is so profoundly involved with everybody else and

4

*in which nobody can really imagine what private guilt can
be anymore.*

According to McLuhan the invention of the printing press changed a tribal society into a fragmented, "linear" society. Such a society, McLuhan believes, is undesirable. People are too individual, isolated, rational, and uninvolved. Television, however, is our savior. Because viewers use two senses, television is a "cool" medium, a medium which maintains a sensory balance rather than stressing one sense at the expense of another. Furthermore, according to McLuhan, television involves us more because a picture on the tube consists of a mosaic of dots which the nervous system must transform into a picture of reality. Because viewers are "involved" in television, McLuhan concludes, society is being transformed into a more involved, "tribal" society. Specialization and fragmentation have given way to mass involvement:

*Print technology created the public. Electric technology
created the mass. The public consists of separate individuals
walking around with separate, fixed points of view. The
new technology demands that we abandon the luxury of
this posture, this fragmentary outlook.* [5]

Here is where McLuhan now seems to be looking in the rear—view mirror. Many theorists doubt that a mass society ever existed, but if it did it is now giving way to a specialized society. And where a mass society was once served by mass media, specialized society is being increasingly served by specialized media.

To understand why the media are becoming specialized it is necessary to have some idea of how people use the

5

media and the effects of the media on people. To do that we will formulate a theory which turns McLuhan on his head: it is not the medium which is the message but the message which is the medium.

THE LOGIC OF McLUHAN

It is difficult to treat McLuhan logically because of his confusing and contradictory style of writing. Those who formulate his ideas into logical propositions, however, generally have little trouble poking holes in McLuhan's argument. Wilbur Schramm, for example, knocks an important leg from under McLuhan's theory that dots on a picture tube explain why television involves us more. In Schramm's words, "If this were so, we should expect the perception of halftones in a newspaper to have the same effect and the perception of type from the dots of a halftone to have an essentially different effect from that of print reproduced by offset or letterpress."[6]

If, however, we ignore the logical inconsistencies in McLuhan's writings and attempt to test his total proposition that television has changed the personalities of people, then we have the basis for scientific investigation of the theory. Skiff and Yarbrough, in Chapter 2, have done just that. They derived a set of logical propositions from McLuhan's writings and developed scales to measure them from a vocational interest test which has been used since the late 1920's. Skiff and Yarbrough then applied the scales to data from three comparative groups of people, collected both before and after the advent of television.

Skiff and Yarbrough found, not that people have become less rational, more intuitive, and more involved, as McLuhan holds, but rather that their personalities have remained "remarkably stable over time". The environment constantly changes, they concluded, but underneath people remain essentially the same.

Even if the media do not change the personalities of individuals, however, they could still change behaviors of people. Any technology, be it automobiles, television or washing machines change patterns of behavior, simply because they open up options which people have not had before. A multi—national study of the ways in which people use their time shows, for example, that people who have television sets spend less time sleeping, in doing household chores, in conversation, and in visiting friends, relatives and neighbors than those who do not have a set.[7] While these effects may seem undesirable to many, they are by no means changes which have rearranged the fabric of society.

Television may allow us to view a war in our living room, be exposed to many additional products, and to gen— erally view places and events we could never see before. These no doubt have effects on the way people react to the places and events. There is much evidence to indicate, however, that not everyone reacts in the same way to what he sees on television. A college student will see the war in his living room quite differently than will an aging veteran, and someone who has used the latest miracle deodorant will view a commercial for that product quite differently from someone who has never used it before.

Here is where we can turn McLuhan on his head. McLuhan says that the "medium is the message", that the technology

7

of the medium makes people and society what they are. Instead, we would say that people and societies face constantly changing environments to which they must adapt. Communication is perhaps the most important behavior which they use to cope with their environment. Media are an extension of people in that media allow people to search a much broader area for relevant information or because the media bring much more unsolicited information in from the environment. People tend to use a medium because they have learned that the medium provides them information which is relevant in given situations. If a medium does not contain a situationally relevant message, it is useless because it constrains an individual's information search or because it provides him with unwanted noise.

Thus, "linear" thinkers tend to extend their communication abilities through the print media because those media contain the information they need. "Tribal" thinkers use television because it contains content which allows escape from alienation and requires little rational thought.

McLuhan and his followers seem to make the mistake of looking at the people who use different media and assuming that the media created the differences in these people. Most communication theorists today, however, reverse this cause and effect relationship. Instead, they look at how people with differing backgrounds, information needs, and shared interests use the media to cope with the environment and how the media constrain or enhance this coping behavior.

MEDIA USE AND MEDIA EFFECTS

Arguments have raged for years over the relationship

8

between the use of the media and the attitudes and values of people. The mass society and the McLuhan approaches represent the early view that media somehow manipulate the "mass mind". That view gave way in the 1950's to the "limited effects" view of the media. That view was based on research which showed that people selectively expose themselves to media and content which reinforce what they want to hear and that media are only one force in a nexus of forces which determine attitudes and values.[8]

One of the significant changes in our understanding of the media came when research began to indicate that the psychological concepts of attitudes and values were of relatively little value in understanding media effects. Instead it became clear that people use the media to form opinions,[9] to discriminate between alternatives in a choice situation,[10] to have something to talk about with other people,[11] or simply to escape from their frustrations.[12] One explanation of these findings comes from the "uses and gratifications approach" to media use. According to this theory, people use the media instrumentally for a variety of "important things", their perceived needs and gratifications.[13]

We can explain this non—attitudinal theory of media use well in terms of concepts from a "coorientation" model of communication developed by Chaffee and McLeod.[14] That model conceptualizes the possible effects of communication between two people. After communicating, two people may agree with one another—i.e., share the same evaluations of (attitudes toward) psychological objects. Or they may simply understand each other better—i.e., be able to

9

comprehend each other's picture of the world even though they may not share the same evaluations of the objects pictured in their minds. There is much evidence to show that communication frequently increases understanding but that it seldom increases agreement.[15] If we extend this model from two people to the relationship between a medium and its audience, then we can say that the media often have the effect of helping people to understand their environment but that the media seldom influence the way people evaluate that environment.

People still use the media selectively, but they do not always, if very often, select messages which reinforce their values, as selective exposure and cognitive dissonance theories hold.[16] Rather, they select those media which are *relevant*— i.e., those media which help people to *understand* problems they face in their environments. From this viewpoint, it should be clear that it is the message which is the medium, not the medium which is the message.

There is also evidence, however, that people sometimes use media purely for diversion and enjoyment and not because the message is relevant to a problem.[17] People once used mass magazines and movies for diversion, but now television is the primary diversionary medium. In other words, the entertainment media generally have been the "mass" media. Some people read or attend to "news media" just for entertainment or to fill time. But more often, they turn to the pure entertainment media, especially television, when they have more time available. Thus, less educated people, who generally devote less time to their jobs and to such activities as clubs and interest groups generally

10

have the most available time and spend it watching tele-vision. [18]

With this background in communication theory, then, we can explain why some mass media are giving way to specialized media and why others are not. To have a mass audience for a mass medium means that individuals with different needs, problems, or preferences all use the same media content, or program, at the same time. There is little evidence to suggest that people ever group together in such a mass when they seek instrumental information about their environments. Pember points out that at one time divergent mass audiences did exist. [19]

In the 1930's, as far as American media merchants were concerned, the audience for newspapers, radio, movies, magazines, and other media was perceived as a single mass...There was evidence to suggest that it was the correct perception of the audience. Mass attendance at the movies was very high. Giant urban daily newspapers maintained circulations above or approaching the millions. Network radio reached tens of millions of listeners each night. Brand-name products attained sales never before dreamed of. Truly, these were mass media, reaching a mass society with a mass culture.

Now, Pember adds, increasing affluence, higher edu-cational levels, and more leisure time have disintegrated the mass audience. Now members of the mass perceive themselves as members of an ethnic group, a region of the country, or an interest group. Or they now have time for

11

particular hobbies and interests. The media, in turn, have responded with specialized content for specialized interests. [20]

Gumpert, in Chapter 5, labels this change in media as "The Rise of Mini—Comm," the expansion of "media of communication which reach specific select audiences,...yet consist of enough people to fit the criteria of a mass audience." In Chapter 6, Maisel reaches the same conclusion, pointing out that a post—industrial society is characterized by service industries "which are great consumers of specialized media." He supports this conclusion with evidence that demand for specialized media, education, entertainment and advertising has been growing at a faster rate than demand for comparable mass media and services.

A cursory examination of television content would suggest that a mass audience still exists for entertainment programs on that medium. But, as Maisel shows, demand for specialized entertainment outside the media, in the theatre for example, is growing at a faster rate than demand for mass entertainment. Therefore, what appears to be a demand for "mass" entertainment on television occurs not because that is what people prefer but because of the economic and technological structure of that medium.

We can best approach this aspect of media effects by first introducing a recent area of communication research dealing with the "agenda—setting function of the media." The agenda—setting function, which has been most researched by McCombs, Shaw, and McLeod, means simply that although the media may not tell people what to think they do tell people what to think about. [21] In short, the decisions made by media gatekeepers essentially set the boundaries which determine those parts of the environment that media audiences will be able to understand.

If the media by design or accident limit their content to certain areas, then people will not be able to adopt, or adapt to, those aspects of the environment which are not placed on the agenda. Agenda setting might explain, for example, why we seldom see good drama on television or thorough coverage of economics in newspapers.

The content of the news media is determined by the judgment of gatekeepers —— i.e., reporters and editors. Those judgments should be made according to the professional criterion of what a medium's audience most wants or most needs to understand about its environment. Often, however, that decision is made in other ways. For the entertainment media, the decision is based largely on the criterion of whether a type of content can attract the kind of audience to which an advertiser would like to sell a product. Those economic decisions largely explain the nature of television content today and to a lesser extent the content of other media.

Opinions on the effect advertising has on media content range from those of people who believe that advertising is "the bulwark of a free press" which has no effect on gatekeeper decisions, to the arguments of radicals who claim that advertisers are the controllers of a vast establishment conspiracy. The best explanation of the relationship between advertising and content would seem to lie between these two extremes. The relationship is a systemic one. Any medium has to have financial support to survive and

13

that support must come from either the government or from a capitalistic system. Therefore, no medium is really "free."

In a capitalistic system, a medium must attract an audience to sell advertising for financial support. But the nature of the advertised product affects the kind of audience that the owner of a medium will attempt to attract. The content of the medium must attract an audience which is likely to buy advertised products.

Put another way, the advertiser, not the viewer or reader is the consumer of a medium, and the product that is sold is not the content of the medium but the audience. Melody explains the relationship as follows for broadcasting:[22]

> The fundamental economic exchange in broadcast markets takes place between the market—manager (network or station) and the advertiser...the market manager brings to the market a product package that will permit an advertiser to reach a a particular audience, e.g. a mass viewing audience of a potential numerical size, or a specialized audience such as housewives, sports fans, or children...The product exchanged between the market manager and the advertiser is access to a wide variety of audiences...Program creation and production is directed toward attracting audiences of particular sizes and compositions that will be increasingly valuable and saleable to advertisers.

The audience for television generally must be a mass audience if the "market—manager" is to be able to sell his product for a price that will allow him to cover the high cost of production and distribution of television programs and provide the highest possible profit. Thus, the "market manager" must appeal to the "lowest common denominator"

14

in the hopes of bringing in a large audience. Although many potential audiences may prefer more specialized television content, no one will provide that kind of content if it cannot draw the size of audience which can be marketed to an advertiser.

The same economics also explains the death of mass magazines and the birth of specialized magazines, the specialization of radio, and the growth of suburban news-papers, media which will be discussed in Part II of this book. In each case the specialized publication attracted an audience that an advertiser was willing to buy and hence these media were able to serve the specialized needs of those audiences.

Fot television, however, technology and economic scar-city constrains the ability of "market-managers to program for specialized audiences. Because of high costs and the limited number of available channels, the broadcast media find they must attempt to create a mass audience during prime time and appeal to specialized audiences only in such hours as Saturday morning (children), late afternoons (housewives), and weekend afternoons (football addicts).

Here, however, is where the new media made possible by the cable and cassettes may allow television to become a more specialized medium that can meet the needs of specialized audiences. New technology offers the possibility of a means of financial support other than advertising (such as pay TV, support from local interest groups, or cassettes borrowed from a library) and would allow many more channels (which takes away the high price that a limited resource always commands). Thus, cable and cassette TV, if properly

15

administered and regulated could bring an end to the last "mass" medium— at least TV would no longer be a predominantly mass medium and Marshall McLuhan's baby will have grown into a mature and more useful adult. Part III of this book will cover these new media in depth.

The last two chapters of Part I examine the future of communication and the media. Clay T. Whitehead, formerly of the White House Office of Telecommunications Policy, examines in Chapter 3 how the constraints of government policy will have to be altered in order to allow the media of the future to best serve the public interest. Policy he says, should free the media from as many regulatory constraints as possible so that they can serve specialized "non-geographic communities of interest". Finally, Ronald Kriss, who has worked with several specialized media, crystal balls future trends in the media.

Part IV of the book then examines the capacity of journalists to produce specialized content which specialized media will have to provide specialized audiences. Generally, the consensus is that the media are becoming specialized more rapidly than are the journalists who staff them.

A VALUE QUESTION

To end this introductory chapter, it is important to examine a value question. Many observers are frightened by the trend toward fragmentation of society and the concomitant growth of specialized media. Many of these observers continue to believe that if only we could communicate with one another through mass media, somehow mass consensus and understanding will be possible. That was the optimistic belief of sociologist Charles Horton Cooley 65 years ago and it is still the hope of many today.[23]

But communication research has shown that communication is only a tool which people can use. It cannot remake people into something better if they do not want it to. People are not homogeneous, and the media will not make them so. One can look at the future more optimistically if he assumes that specialized media will meet the individual needs of "non-geographic communities of interest" and that these media will allow people to be more individual and less dependent on a few non-specialized sources of information.

Many fear, for example, that if cable television makes it possible for people to shop, attend local government meetings, or attend an opera at home that we will become a society of recluses. Some people may withdraw inward, but others may use the new media to gain more time for leisure activities, access to meetings that they may never have had time to attend, and the financial capability of receiving entertainment never before within their means.

Hence we return to the theme of turning McLuhan on his head. The important value question is not what the media do to people but how people themselves choose to use the media. Specialized media will allow many more individuals a wider choice of the media they use. This individual freedom should increase, and the manipulative power of the media should decline. But only if we choose not to be manipulated.

1. Marshall McLuhan and Quentin Fiore, *The Medium is the Message* (New York; Bantam Books, 1967), pp. 74–75.

2. Elihu Katz and Paul F. Lazarsfeld, *Personal Influence* (Glencoe, Ill.; The Free Press, 1955).

3. Dennis McQuail, *Towards a Sociology of Mass Communications* (London: Collier–MacMillan, 1969), pp. 56–57; Charles K. Atkin, "*Instrumental Utilities and Information Seeking,*" in Peter Clarke (ed.), *New Models for Mass Communication Research* (Beverly Hills: Sage Publications, 1973), pp. 205–242; Steven H. Chaffee and Jack M. Mcleod, "Individual vs. Social Predictors of Information Seeking," *Journalism Quarterly* 50 (1973): 237–245.

4. McLuhan and Fiore, Op. cit., p. 61.

5. *Ibid*, pp. 68–69.

6. Wilbur Schramm, *Men, Messages, and Media* (New York: Harper & Row, 1973), pp. 125–129.

7. John P. Robinson, "Television's Impact on Everyday Life: Some Cross-national Evidence," *In Television and Social Behavior*, Vol. 4, A Technical Report to the Surgeon General's Scientific Advisory Committee on Television and Social Behavior, p. 427.

8. An approach generally identified with Joseph T. Klapper. *The Effects of Mass–Communication* (New York: The Free Press, 1960).

9. Richard F. Carter, Ronald H. Pyszka and Jose L. Guerrero, "Dissonance and Exposure to Aversive Information," *Journalism Quarterly* 46 (1969): 37–42.

10. James E. Grunig, "A Decision–Situation Model of Communication Behavior", paper presented to the Association for Education in Journalism, Fort Collins, Colo., August 1973.

11. Chaffee and McLeod, *op. cit.*

12. Kline, for example, found use of television to be strongly related to interpersonal alienation which in turn was negatively related to education and income. F. Gerald Kline, "Media Time Budgeting as a Function of Demographics and Lifestyle," *Journalism Quarterly* 48 (1971): 211–221.

13. Elihu Katz, Jay G. Blumler, and Michael Gurevitch, "Uses and Gratifications Research," *Public Opinion Quarterly* 37 (1973); Elihu Katz, Michael Gurevitch and H. Haas, On the Use of Mass Media for Important Things," *American Sociological Review* 38 (1973): 164–181.

14. Jack M. McLeod and Steven H. Chaffee, "Interpersonal Approaches to Communication Research," *American Behavioral Scientist* 16 (1973): 469–499.

15. Daniel B. Wackman, "Interpersonal Communication and Coorientation," *American Behavioral Scientist* 16 (1973): 537–550.

16. Richard F. Carter, "The Alchemy of Communication," Paper presented to the Association for Education in Journalism, Berkeley, Calif., August 1969; Jonathan L. Freedman and David O. Sears, "Selective Exposure," in Leonard Berkowitz (ed.) *Advances in Experimental Social Psychology*, Vol. 2 (New York: Academic Press, 1965), pp. 58–98.

17. William Stephenson, *The Play Theory of Mass Communication* (Chicago: University of Chicago Press, 1967).

18. Merrill Samuelson, Richard F. Carter and Lee Ruggels, "Education, Available Time, and Use of Mass Media," *Journalism Quarterly* 40 (1963): 491–496.

19. Don R. Pember, *Mass Media in America* (Chicago: Science Research Associates, 1974), pp. 331–332.

20. *Ibid.*

21. Maxwell McCombs and Donald L. Shaw, "A Progress

19

Report on Agenda—Setting Research,''Paper presented to the Association for Education in Journalism, San Diego, Calif., August 1974; Jack M. McLeod, Lee B. Becker, and James E. Byrnes, "Another Look at the Agenda—Setting Function of the Press," *Communication Research* 1 (1974): 131—166.

22. William Melody, *Children's Television: The Economics of Exploitation* (New Haven: Yale University Press, 1973), pp. 13—14.

23. Charles H. Cooley, *Social Organization* (New York: Charles Scribner & Sons, 1909).

2

DOES COMMUNICATION TECHNOLOGY CHANGE PEOPLE?
Some Empirical Evidence on McLuhan's "Global V llage"

Donald E. Skiff and J. Paul Yarbrough

That the world is changing, and ever more swiftly, is undeniable. That the changes are inevitably beneficient to man is not so certain. What technology does *to* man is as important a question as what it does *for* him. Some argue that man is basically unchanged by the alteration of his world but others are saying that man is losing his humanness in the furious race to the future, and that he is becoming like the machines he creates. The world is changing, but the question remains: is man?

Still another voice has been raised. Man *is* changed by his environment, says Marshall McLuhan, and he *has* taken the shape of the mechanical, linear, fragmented world he has created. But there is something more. His most recent technology––electricity––is making him over again. Electric media of communication are reversing the trend toward the mechanical man that was impelled by typography and the print media, back toward the whole man, the intuitive man, the tribal man.

In the uncertainty that seems the most prominent characteristic of our age, McLuhan's ideas are bound to attract attention and controversy. His oracular style of writing contributes to the heat of the argument, but unfortunately does little to clarify the issues. To examine the ideas of McLuhan one must first know what it is that he is saying. Translation of another man's words carries a two-edged risk: one may be mistaken about what the other man is saying, and one may be too inarticulate to express it. Mindful of this danger, we have attempted to put McLuhan's ideas into a systematic form, and to test certain aspects of his claims.

Beginning with assumptions about the essential nature of man and how he tries to control his environment, the cause-and-effect relationship in McLuhan's theories can be traced from purposeful behavior to consequences to responses, both as conscious adaptation and as mental conditioning. According to McLuhan, communications media ––and other technologies functioning incidentally as communications media––occupy a central place in this interplay. In the end, the nature of the dominant media changes man's sensory balance and thereby changes how and what he perceives. The effect is threefold: the nature of the media affects the way man perceives his environment, the way he organizes cognitive data, and the way he relates to people and the events around him.

Because of electric media, McLuhan says, and especially because of television, people in our society are becoming less analytical, less methodical––less "rational"––and more "intuitive" in their perceptions. They are becoming less compartmentalized, "fragmented" and more "integrated" in their thinking. They are becoming more "involved" in people and causes, less "detached" and isolated.

If what McLuhan says is true, then the changes that are occurring in people should be observable in how they respond to aspects of their environment. More specifically, if people are changing in the way he says they are, we should expect them to express different preferences for activities and occupations since the introduction and diffusion of television than they did before this influence began. They should prefer those activities and occupations that are more compatible with their changed natures.

According to McLuhan, television has had, and is having, a pronounced effect upon the society and its members. In only 20 years, he says, we are different. If what he says is true, then that difference should be revealed in how we respond to various aspects of our environment, compared with a time before the advent of television.

It would be easy enough to build psychological tests which would measure—today—our responses to the environment along the dimensions McLuhan discusses. The problem, of course, is to find some way of measuring responses of people *before* the introduction of television.

Since the changes McLuhan writes about can be considered personality characteristics, they should be inferable from the results of some kind of personality inventory. Fortunately, during the past several decades a number of standardized personality tests have been administered to large numbers of people. Data from one of these tests could be used to test McLuhan's hypothesis if the tests had been administered to equivalent groups of people over a time

23

span covering the introduction and absorption of television into the cultural mileau.

The *Strong Vocational Interest Blank* (SVIB), one of these personality inventories, was selected as both a source of data and as an instrument from which scales could be developed to measure the dimensions of personality McLuhan claims are changing.

The SVIB is a 400–item questionnaire comprised of 280 names of occupations, school subjects, amusements, activities, and peculiarities of people to which the subject responds "like," "indifference," or "dislike." It also includes 40 items requiring an ordering of preference among groups of related activities, 40 items calling for a comparison of interest between pairs of items, and 40 items asking for an evaluation of the subject's own characteristics.

The SVIB was first used in 1927 and was based on the discovery that different groups of professional people showed consistent differences in what they said they liked and disliked. Many of these differences concerned things with no apparent occupational connection. E. K. Strong built the test by comparing the likes and dislikes of various occupational groups with those of people in general and by deriving scales for each group. Subjects could then be tested with the SVIB and profiles drawn showing how their interests compared with the averages in each of the occupational groups.

Research on the SVIB has shown that these interest profiles are stable over time for most people. The interest profiles also generally develop before a person enters an

24

occupation, which indicates that these patterns are part of the personality and are not generated by participation in an occupation.

Items were selected from the SVIB to measure the three McLuhan concepts of personality. Selection was based, first, on value judgements of a panel of three judges, then by a forward—solution cluster analysis. "Rationality" and "intuitiveness" were first believed to be polar opposites on a single dimension, but the analysis showed them to be two weakly, but positively, correlated scales. "Involvement," the feeling of dealing with people rather than things, became the third scale.

Three different sample populations were selected from those for which SVIB data were available: entering students at the University of Minnesota College of Liberal Arts, high school seniors in rural Minnesota schools, and a collection of adult professional—managerial occupation groups, all having comparable item response data from across the time period covering the introduction and development of television. The scales were applied to the item responses of the three groups, at three points in time for the two student groups and at four points for the adult group.

Two general hypotheses guided the analysis of the data:

1. The prediction that people who have been exposed to television will score higher on all three tribal scales (low rationality, high intuitiveness, and high involvement).

2. The prediction that the rate of change in scores will be greater for young people who have been exposed to television during their formative years than for adults who were not exposed to television during their formative years.

25

Table 1 shows the mean scores for each of the three sample groups for each of the scales and time periods measured. Note that the rational scale has been scored negatively; a high numerical score indicates less rational orientation. This was done so that high scores on all three scales would represent a high degree of "tribalism," the quality toward which McLuhan says television is moving society.

Figure 1 shows the distribution of the scores for the three samples on the rational scale. An analysis of variance shows that only for the high school sample is there a statistically significant trend in the direction proposed by McLuhan. That mean score, however, increased only 1.47 points from 1947 to 1963 in a possible range of 35 points.

To test the second general hypothesis on the rationality scale, the rates of increase for the college and high school students were compared with the rate of increase for the adult sample. There was no significant difference between the rate of increase for the college and adult samples. The rate of increase was significantly higher for the high school group as compared to the adult group, but only because the scores of the adult group declined over this period.

Figure 2 shows the distribution of scores on the intuitive scale. In this case there was a statistically significant increase only for the adult sample, and this was an increase of .80 points in a possible range of 28 points. No significant differences were found in the rates of change of the two youth samples as compared with the adult sample.

Finally, Figure 3 shows the distribution of data for the
26

involved scale. On this scale, no significant differences in scores over time and in rates of change were found.

In total, two general hypotheses testing McLuhan's theories were tested on three sample populations——resulting in 15 empirical hypotheses or statistical comparisons. Of the 15 comparisons, only three showed a statistically significant difference. And these few differences represented small changes on the scale ranges involved. Therefore, both general hypotheses must be rejected.

Rejection of these hypotheses could mean either that McLuhan is wrong or that this test of McLuhan's theories was inadequate. First, McLuhan could be wrong. Man may not be changing from his exposure to television; he may not be changing at all. He may not be changing in the way McLuhan says. Or, he may be affected, not by the nature of the medium, but by the particular content of the medium, controlled by groups of people who happen to be oriented toward the world in a certain way. Perhaps the most intriguing finding of the study was the remarkable stability of personality orientation over time for samples from three disparate populations, in the midst of a rapidly changing environment.

Alternatively, however, the assumptions behind the selection of the SVIB as an instrument capable of testing the subtle personality characteristics in question may be wrong. The items of the SVIB may not be sensitive enough to detect changes of the magnitude that may actually exist. Yet, several researchers have related the SVIB to other, more deeply probing, inventories with substantial correlation. Also, McLuhan claims that the changes are not subtle but very marked. The SVIB has been shown to be highly predictive, which is not a superficial quality in test design.

The method of selecting the items for the scales may also have been inadequate. A different panel of judges might have made different decisions, affecting the final selection of scale items and possibly the pattern of test scores themselves. On the other hand, the scales developed were highly reliable (with reliability coefficients in the range of .80 to .90 from comparable populations at three points in time). So, while the validity of the scales might be questioned, reliability should not be a problem.

Sampling error could be another possible explanation of the negative results. But using three sample groups from different populations should have minimized the probability of sampling error. Finally, the selection of only three or four points in time could have created too sparse a population on which to plot curves or calculate trends.

Given these alternative explanations, it seems inappropriate to express strong conclusions about what the test results mean. But given the facts revealed by these manipulations, we must reject McLuhan's claim that the perceptual, cognitive, and relating faculties of people are being changed by television. If we accept his assertion that these changes are profound and far—reaching, we should expect to have revealed them with the instrument and the method used.

Men change their behavior to deal with a world that is constantly changing, and those behavioral changes become patterns of living. It is possible, however, that beneath

28

these changing patterns men remain pretty much the same. At the level of conscious choice, of adaptation, change is obvious. But McLuhan contends that technologies—media——change the nature of man. If he is right, we have not demonstrated it.

TABLE 1

MEAN SCORES FOR THREE McLUHAN SCALES

	SCALE		
Sample Group	Rational[1]	Intuitive	Involved
University students			
1949	33.74	28.38	32.53
1958	30.64	26.66	30.31
1967	32.18	29.65	32.53
High school students			
1948	30.47	23.31	27.06
1957	30.83	21.28	26.27
1963	31.94	21.36	27.52
Adults			
1927–39	31.85	29.04	30.96
1940–51	31.44	28.72	31.83
1952–64	31.79	31.94	33.32
1965–66	30.75	29.52	31.84

[1] High scores indicate low rationality.

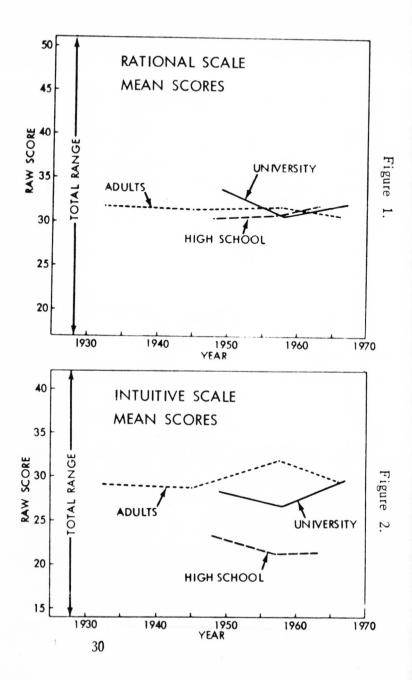

RATIONAL SCALE
MEAN SCORES

Figure 1.

INTUITIVE SCALE
MEAN SCORES

Figure 2.

30

Figure 3.

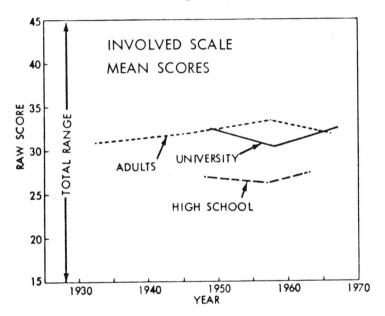

3

COMMUNICATION AND THE FUTURE

Clay T. Whitehead

In my days at the Rand Corporation I worked with a number of people who were trying to predict what America would be like in the year 2000 (or the year 1976 for some studies). Being a bit of a cynic, I compared some earlier projections with what had actually materialized. Generally, we came to the conclusion that predicting 25 years into the future was totally impossible. When we projected 10 years into the future, which is just far enough to see something interesting, the error rate approached something like 95%. On the other hand, when you predict only one year in the future, people remember what you projected, so that was not one of the most popular areas of projection at places like Rand.

When I became an advisor in the White House, I began to think about communications policy, which to me meant asking how we regulate communication in this country, what kind of communications we want in the future, and what objectives we want our communications systems to serve. I found very little consensus on these questions.

So rather than attempting to predict here how communications will develop in the future, I will simply try to provide my perspective on the factors that will guide the development of communications and hope that this will help you draw your own conclusions about the future of communications.

Much of the popular discussion of communications in the future centers on Marshall McLuhan's concept of a global village. Everyone in the world, or at least everyone in this country, has access to much the same kind of information. Yet the theme of this book is specialized communications, the media of the future. Superficially there might seem to be conflict between a global village and specialized communication, but I think that the exact opposite is true. In the global village, or at least in American village, we are finding a whole host of new communities, non-geographic communities of shared interests, which desperately need communications. By definition we are talking about specialized communications. This kind of specialized communications among non-geographic communities will be the predominant theme of communication in this country in the future.

Likewise, more and more of our communications in this country will be electronic. I am not sounding the death knell to the *Baltimore Sun* or to print journalism, but am simply saying that electronics is and will be playing a much larger role in the future. Already the lines between electronic and print communications are blurring. We have long distance xerography utilizing the telephone lines. We have telex. And right now the Dow-Jones Company distributes the *Wall Street Journal* across the country by microwave to be printed on remote printing presses.

Since World War II, there has been a tremendous outburst of creativity and development in electronics, but unfortunately most of this creativity and development have not found their way into electronic communications. There are two big, big forces retarding experiment and growth in electronic communications.

The first is the federal government and the 1934 Communications Act. By virtue of that act, which I presume made sense in its day, no electronic communication service of any kind can be offered in this country without the prior approval of the Federal Communications Commission. The FCC asks the would-be entrepreneur to prove that a service is worthwhile, economical, and that the public wants it before he is allowed to even try. Obviously, such a policy discourages innovation.

The second force retarding innovation in electronic communications is monopoly, which is very much a characteristic of private business in the electronic communications field today. The American Telephone and Telegraph Company monopolizes the common carrier field; the three television networks in the television field.

Those with corporate interests argue that the United States has the best television system in the world. Indeed, they say the status quo in communications in this country is the optimum communications system for the future. I agree that we do have the best television system and the best telephone system. But it is precisely because we do have the best in the world that we in this country have the ability as no other country in this world to look beyond basic telephone service, to look beyond a basic level of national mass television service, and to look to a whole host of new and specialized communications for non-geographic communities of interest.

The telephone business today has a lot in common with the automobile business. For years and years the only Ford that you could buy was a black "Model T". The same was also true with the telephone. Today both the telephone business and the automobile business offer a proliferation of colors and models and a lot of optional equipment. But they offer precious little real choice and precious little competition in providing totally different kinds of communications equipment such as data and facsimile computer terminals in the home. Imagine plugging one of those new little electronic calculators into your telephone––from there into the computer––from there into the college––from there into a friend's home––from there to your bank. Then imagine remote access to libraries.

All of that is technically possible and appears to be economically feasible. But none of it is going to come until we have some competition in common carrier communications similar to the competition of foreign companies in the automobile business.

In the television industry, it is difficult to believe that the public interest in this country can possibly be served by freezing the number of TV channels that we have today, and by blocking the growth of cable television which could greatly expand the number of TV channels. Yet that is exactly what the broadcast industry and the three television networks are telling us today. In their view we can have quality television only by preserving the present limited

35

number of channels. I think exactly the opposite is true. Cable television has to be allowed to grow on an economic basis, as a medium co—equal with broadcasting. It has to have its own regulatory framework passed by the Congress. It has to develop not just as television, but rather as a new medium encouraged to have a diversity of programming and a multitude of channels. Then each of us would have much more choice in what we can see and hear.

In short, the world of the future is going to need more communications, it is going to need lower cost communications. And one way or another the great institutions——the United States Government, the phone company and the three television networks——are going to have to change in order to permit that to come about.

Now let us ask what this means for journalism and the media. The media today differ in two important ways from what they were in the past, and from the kind of media that so much of our theory of government—media relations is based on. The first big difference is that the media in this country have become big business, and in many ways monopolistic. A very limited number of television stations around the country are principally programmed by·three New York City television stations——i.e., three television networks. We have fewer and fewer newspapers each year, With a limited number of TV stations, with a shrinking number of papers, and with TV stations often owned by a newspaper in the community, we find fewer and fewer media voices available to each of us as citizens.

The second big difference is that government regulation of the content of television broadcasting has steadily expanded to the point where today federal bureaucracy administers a pervasive system of controls over what we see and hear on television. This is a situation far different from what we are accustomed to seeing in the print media. The FCC already has 15 favored categories of programming, and now it is talking about setting minimum percentages of these categories that each television station in the nation would have to program in order to keep its license. With the tremendous profits in television broadcasting, it would take either a very stupid or very courageous broadcaster to not conform to what the FCC wants in the way of programming.

We have a Fairness Doctrine, which is now something similar to what motherhood was before zero population growth. No one opposes fairness; but what is fairness in the media when it is decided by a government bureaucracy? One must worry about censorship when a government agency seriously tries to decide which issues are of public importance, how many sides there are to each of those issues, who qualifies as a legitimate spokesman, and whether or not each of those sides on each of those issues has received adequate coverage. Similarly, one must be concerned about the FCC's Prime Time Access Rule which allows a government agency to tell a local station which hours of which days of the week it can broadcast, which kinds of programming it can take from the network, and which programs can be produced locally or bought from syndicated sources.

In short, we have today a system of government control of what we see and hear that seems totally at odds with

37

the First Amendment of the Constitution. How did that come to be? Originally, this kind of regulation was based on the concept that because broadcasters use the public airwaves and because there are a limited number of those airwaves, that the government has some obligation to see how they are used on behalf of the public. But more and more rationale in FCC decisions has shifted subtly away from the use of the public airwaves and shifted to the rationale that there is a scarcity of broadcast stations available. When scarcity becomes the rationale for the federal government deciding about the appropriateness of media programming, then we have to look rather nervously over our shoulder at what is happening in the newspaper business. There are already fewer daily newspapers in this country than radio stations. In many communities there are more television stations than newspapers. In short, the scarcity rationale applies directly to newspapers. When you consider the joint ownership of many newspapers and television stations in particular markets, you begin to see scarcity with a vengeance.

Many people in this country would like to see a Fairness Doctrine for newspapers. They would like to see an equal space requirement in the newspapers just like we have an equal time requirement in broadcasting. If scarcity is the only reason for government regulation of the content of the media, there will be no shortage of self—appointed overseers of the public interest who will prove scarcity to justify using government to get attention to their point of view in each of the media.

All of us must ask ourselves if we really believe that

a bureaucratically—administered press is a free press——even though we might approve of some of the results of some of that FCC regulation, even if we might like to see poor people get free space in a newspaper to answer an editorial. In my judgment there is no such thing as a slightly-administered system of censorship——be it negative censorship to get the media to delete certain types of coverage or be it the equally pernicious positive censorship, whereby the government requires the media to give prominent attention to favored points of view.

The big challenge in the communications field for the next few years is to make sure that we have a free electronic press and that we keep our free print press. The big challenge to a free press will not come from a number of special assistants in the White House who seem demonstratively lacking in judgment and who skirt the edge of illegality in using government processes to coerce the media into providing coverage. We are seeing today that people who lack the judgment to refrain from breaking the law to achieve those ends will be caught.

The real threat is the year by year, perfectly legal, accumulation of control by the FCC and the Courts——all for the best causes, all for the public interest——of what actually goes out over the airwaves. Reversing the trend of the last 10 years of creeping FCC controls over what our electronic media are programming will require concentrated effort in the government by journalists (be they print or be they in the electronic media), and a lot of public support. I am not sure that the press establishment in this country can demonstrate the concentrated effort and attention needed to gain public support, but that is what is necessary.

The problem of justifying governmental interference applies with a vengeance to cable television. In cable there seems to be no need to compromise the public interest and the private interest. Properly regulated, cable television requires no use of the airwaves, therefore no rationale for government oversight. There would be no scarcity of channels, therefore no need to ration who gets access. Cable also promises low cost. All this adds up to no excuse in cable television for the government to control the use or the content of channels as long as we simply assure that everyone has access to those channels, just as everyone today has access to the use of printing presses and to the use of the mail.

But when we have slowed the trend towards governmental specification of television programming...when cable television has come and brought lots of television channels and when the government has no authority over how those channels are programmed...when the battle for real press freedom is won and we have a free electronic press just as we have a free print press...when the government has no legal way to compel fairness, competence, judgment, accuracy and so forth on the part of the professional journalist...then when that nirvana arrives, where does journalism go?

This country consists of a government, an economy, and a society of checks and balances. The press loves to talk about itself as a vital check on government and of course it is. The conscientious, professional journalist is a guardian of the public interest. But yet in the year 2000 the central question of a free press in a free society is the question originally asked nearly 2,000 years ago, ''Who is to guard the guardians?''

40

4

THE MEDIA OF THE FUTURE

Ronald P. Kriss

It takes a special act of courage for someone to discuss the media of the future after he has been directly involved in the death not only of a world wide news service, but also of an entire family of magazines.

Nevertheless, I remain reasonably optimistic about the future of the media...even though I saw International News Service collapse under me in 1958 when I was in Tokyo... even though I was a more than casually interested witness to the death of *Life* magazine in 1973...even though, when I was staffing *Saturday Review*, some of the most talented people I hired were survivors from the shipwreck of *Look*, the shake—up at *Harper's*, and a variety of other communica—tions catastrophes...and even though the new *Saturday Review* itself, one of the more interesting and innovative concepts in recent years, ran out of cash in 1973. But, more about that later.

In his annual President's Report Derek Bok of Harvard noted that, more and more, the nation's universities will be expected to ''supply the knowledge and insight that a complex, troubled society requires." The media—by which I'm talking about newspapers, magazines, radio and television—will certainly be expected to perform the same function— but for a far larger and more diffuse audience.

The media will have certain advantages. Literacy will increase, despite the problems that our schools face. In the closing decades of the twentieth century we will be living in what Peter Drucker, the management analyst, calls "the knowledge society." Even before this decade is over, the knowledge sector"—teachers and scientists, technicians and journalists, government workers and business executives—will account for half of America's Gross National Product. To quote from Drucker's book, *The Age of Discontinuity:* "Every other dollar earned and spent in the American economy will be earned by producing and distributing ideas and information." Lest you think that Mr. Drucker is out on a very shaky limb, his prediction is substantially echoed by John Kenneth Galbraith in *The New Industrial State* and by Daniel Bell in his newly published book, *The Coming of the Post-Industrial Society.* As Mr. Bell notes, this society will be run by an intellectual class whose claim to rule, and whose source of power, will be knowledge rather than capital.

So there will be an immense number of people who will be hungry for information, even dependent on it for their very livelihoods. Much of the information will be technical and narrow—research reports, academic studies, computer print-outs, inter-office memos. But with so literate a society there will inevitably be a great hunger, for more general information about the world at large, and the principal purveyor of this information will be, as it is today, the media.

42

Let's look briefly at the media today. In the U.S. alone there are 1,774 newspapers—although, sad to say, probably 1,750 of them are in localities where there is no competition. There are an astounding number of magazines—10,500 if you count only those that come out at least quarterly, 60,000 if you include those that appear only once or twice a year. In the field of medicine alone, there are no fewer than 350 publications. There are 650 television stations and 4,000 radio stations in this country as well.

If you look at the *whole* communications industry—and that includes ad agencies, public relations firms, direct mail houses and photographic outfits as well as the other media—it's a $60 billion—a—year business that employs half a million people.

It's a giant industry, in short, and its growth in the future is likely to be exponential. Sure, more newspapers will fold and more magazines will fail; only last week, *Intellectual Digest* became the most recent victim.

Still, Marshall McLuhan notwithstanding, the printed word remains a powerful, extraordinarily flexible and relatively inexpensive means of communication—and that guarantees that the press will continue to exert tremendous influence on all our lives. As for T.V., it scarcely needs saying that its future is virtually unlimited.

*   *   *

Technologically, the changes that are coming before the end of this century in the techniques of transmitting and delivering news are likely to add up to a revolution, nothing less. In some city rooms, newsmen already use cathode ray tubes to type and edit their stories. Similarly, optical scanners, leased computer lines, data—speed machines that handle bursts of more than 1,000 words per minute, laser beams hooked to computers—all will be brought into play. There are two chief obstacles to their adoption—costs, which are steadily being reduced; and unions, which are fighting to protect their members that are being forced, more and more, to yield to the new gadgetry. When newspapers are able to take full advantage of these and other innovations, it is estimated that they will be able to reduce their production costs by as much as 50%. Just how significant that figure is, can be seen in the fact that 42% of *The New York Times's* total expenses are devoted to production. Of course, we can hope that some of the savings will be plowed back into editorial operations—but we can't assume that. A. J. Liebling once noted: "The monopoly publisher's reaction on being told that he ought to spend money on reporting distant events, is exactly that of the proprietor of a large, fat cow, who is told he ought to enter her in a horse race."

If anything, the impact of new processes will be even greater on electric journalism. Within our lifetimes, satellite transmissions, video—cassettes and, above all, cable television will revolutionize the field. Right now, roughly six million American homes—10% of all homes with TV—are wired for cable. It was once thought that 50% or even 60% would be hooked into cable by 1980. But the immense costs of laying cable in densely populated urban areas and intense opposition from established TV stations everywhere have delayed our becoming a "wired nation." Still, that revolution will come one day, and when it does, the results will be mind—boggling. In the words of Nicholas Johnson, the former gadfly of the Federal Communications Commission, "coaxial cable is to a telephone wire what Niagara Falls is to a garden hose." At present, most communities have no more than five or six usable channels for TV transmission. Cable will multiply that figure to 20 or 40 or even more channels.

Imagine what that will mean in a field where the costliest programs are usually carried at the highest level—that is, the national level—and aimed at the lowest level, the notorious "lowest common denominator." Cultural events that have been shunned as too difficult or limited in appeal or whatever will finally get an airing. Small communities will be able to reserve several channels for themselves to televise anything from public service announcements to town council meetings. Minorities that have long complained about their lack of access to the media will be able to schedule regular telecasts. A heightened sense of community could result—and I emphasize "could" because there's no guarantee that more than a handful of people will watch any of these high—minded productions.

This abundance of channels is only the beginning. Stuart Sucherman, a Ford Foundation expert on CATV, put it this way: "By installing a strip of copper wire within an insulating sheath only slightly larger in diameter than a lipstick tube, one can bring to every home two—way,

45

broad—band communications that can provide a whole galaxy of new services." Among them: facsimile reproduction of documents, even newspapers and magazines; links with libraries and information banks at universities and medical centers; home fire and crime protection systems; even shopping services by means of links with similarly wired supermarkets.

*   *   *

All of this technological wizardry will open the way to new opportunities—and hazards—for journalists. Erik Erikson wrote in *Young Luther:* "Everything expanding opens frontiers, every conquest exposes flanks." What flanks will be exposed as the communications field expands and conquers?

One danger—a danger that is already severe and getting worse—is the irresistable, tidal flood of information that will be washing over all of us. Merely to keep up, a person must spend so much time ingesting material that he risks having no time left to digest it—to think about it, weigh it, make value decisions on it. I'm afraid that there's just no way to avoid this danger. The most effective individuals of the future, particularly in our field, will be those who are sufficiently disciplined and sufficiently wise to reject— to edit out, in effect—whatever is redundant, or superfluous,

46

or second—rate. Far less effective will be those who are capable of absorbing huge amounts of material and who, like computers, are capable of giving an accurate printout of what they have stored—but are incapable of making sound judgments.

A second danger is that it will become increasingly difficult for the individual journalist to cope with this data explosion, much less to master it. As things are today, the journalist is not exactly the most popular fellow in town. The Harris Poll ranks him below teachers and preachers, bankers and businessmen, doctors and generals, and even below Congressmen. Thomas Griffith, the last editor of *Life* dwells on this in a book he calls *How True: A Skeptics Guide to Believing the News*. Mr. Griffith writes: "In popular judgment, to be a journalist is to be a man slightly suspect, a perverter of truth, an invader of privacy, a disturber of the peace, a sensationalist, a simplifier." Jean—Louis Servan—Schreiber, a leading French writer and publisher, zeroes in on another, related problem. In his book, *The Power to Inform,* he writes: "The journalist is by definition slightly informed on a multitude of subjects; the brief time in which he has to absorb information means that, although the public might regard him as a specialist, he is more often a moron in the eyes of experts."

Them's fightin' words—but too often true. The best way to give them the lie is for journalists to be smarter and harder—working, but that's easier said than done. A few, with extraordinary abilities, will be able to pass muster with the experts in a multiplicity of fields. Most, however, will have to concentrate on developing a particular specialty and keeping abreast of it—even when, as so often happens in the world of a newsroom, they are diverted into other areas. Of course, the need to specialize does not relieve the journalist—any more than it relieves the surgeon or the systems engineer—of his responsibility for knowing what is going on in the rest of the world.

The subject of specialization calls to mind a limerick I heard recently—a clean one, I fear:

> *A certain young lady of Rees*
> *Had a surfeit of Ph.Ds.*
> *Said her doctor: "My dear, it's perfectly clear,*
> *That you're killing yourself with degrees."*

I guess it's evident that I have a certain bias toward the generalist. Perhaps that's because everyone likes to fancy himself capable of covering anything, of being a super—generalist. Or perhaps it's because I'm now primarily an editor—and while an editor may know less about every subject than his writers, he is expected to know enough to be able to assign priorities and to fit things into a larger context. As Max Ways, who was long the resident philosopher at *Fortune* magazine puts it: "The responsibility of the generalist...is to integrate and transcend the specialist, in a continuous process of changing options and evolving purposes."

*   *   *

This is not to say that specialization will not play

an increasingly important role, not only in the education of journalists, but also in the conception of new publications. Of all the magazines launched in recent years (and I exclude the skin mags from this discussion), the few that have survived have almost invariably been specialized journals—either in subject matter, as *Psychology Today,* or in the geographic area covered, as *New York* magazine.

Of course there have been spectacular failures in this effort, and *Saturday Review* was among the most spectacular. The magazine was purchased from Norton Simon in mid–1971 and not long after that its long–time editor, Norman Cousins, departed; he did not see eye to eye with the new owners, two bright but brash entrepreneurs who had made a bundle on *Psychology Today*. What the new owners proposed to do was to split Cousins' weekly magazine into four monthlies covering the arts, education, the society and the sciences. The effort failed for several reasons. The owners wanted too much, too soon; they started with a magazine whose weekly circulation was roughly 650,000 and which sold for 50 cents, and aimed at an average circulation of 750,000 for each of the four monthlies, which sold for $1 per copy. This could only have been done with immense expenditures on direct mail, and with the time to let the concept grow on the readers. As it was, the money ran out before circulation goals could be reached, before the new magazines had a chance to evolve editorially and before Madison Avenue, that purveyor of new detergents, new breakfast cereals, and new cars, had the time to get over its innate horror of anything new in the editorial sphere. Actually, I think the fatal mistake came before all that.

49

When you're trying to do something as radically different as launching a family of four specialized yet related magazines, you should start absolutely fresh. It was wrong to try doing it by reshaping an old, established—some would say fusty—magazine whose readers hated to see *anything* about it change (sometimes, I was inclined to think, even the date).

Time, of course, is in a far different position. Through computerization, it is able to produce scores of different editions—for doctors, business executives, students—but the difference is in the advertising, not the editorial content. This is standard in all domestic editions, and *Time* is an unabashedly general magazine. Because the world grows increasingly complex, I think there will be a need for some time, for the sort of magazine that attempts to cover the whole world, in a bite—sized chunk, for the reader. And yet *Time* and other magazines face a difficult problem: some events are so complex that it takes more and more room to report them with any sort of depth; yet *Time* is reluctant to add pages out of proper concern that it will begin losing readers whose circuits are already dangerously overloaded with data. This means a weekly struggle to fit what is important news into a mere 135 or 140 columns; it also means a weekly bloodbath when the time comes to throw out some excellent stories for lack of space. In some ways, this is not an altogether bad thing: the best, and best—told, stories survive.

*   *   *

In looking to the future, we can readily see that there will be an abundance of outlets—printed and electronic—for the news. It's not as easy to forecast how good, or bad, they will be. Tom Griffith issues this warning in his forth-coming book: "Between networks hobbled by government regulations and newspapers and magazines that are being rendered more cautious by economic considerations, the future of vigorous American journalism, as opposed to the journalism of play safe, is much more precarious, much more dependent on a few brave spirits, than is generally recog-nized." The point is well—taken. When the price of a big metropolitan daily gets up into the $100 million range, the only buyers are likely to be large newspaper chains or corporations. The editors are likely to be chosen on the basis of corporate—not creative—qualities. This hardly bodes well for any sort of fresh groundbreaking, or responsible muckraking. Maybe the answer lies in the growing clout of the journalists' committees that have begun to spring up on European newspapers and are likely to follow here. As for TV, some hard thinking lies ahead about the whole area of government regulation—and intervention. This is particularly true of the fairness doctrine, which could be applied so rigorously that watching documentaries will get to be like watching tennis matches—a stroke to this side and a stroke to the other.

51

*   *   *

When futurologists make their forecasts, they hedge their bets by citing something called the "surprise factor"—which could upset all the others. I'm sure a great number of surprises lie ahead in communications; after all, the industry went through one revolution in the last generation with TV and appears to be on the threshhold of another. One forecast, though, seems fairly surprise–proof—that the future in our field will be anything but dull.

PART II. SPECIALIZED MEDIA TODAY

Too often we are led to believe that the media of public communication in the United States today are mass media because we too often think of television as the predominant medium. But as Honan has shown, for example, more Americans listen to radio each day than watch television.[1] Many observers also cite statistics from national surveys which show that people say they get most of their news from television and thet they say television is the most credible news medium. Yet when people are asked not where they get most of their news but instead where they go for a specific piece of information they generally mention newspapers more often than television.[2] Television, then, is probably an atypical medium because it is the primary remaining unspecialized medium. It too, however, may soon become a specialized medium.

Magazines are perhaps the most specialized of all the media today. This specialization began with the death of mass circulation magazines, a phenomenon caused largely by the loss of mass audience advertising revenues to television. According to Pember, the day of the mass circulation magazine was followed by the "magazine revolution of the sixties" in which "magazines of all shapes and sizes have been founded in an effort to cope with the expanding interests of the reading public.[3]

Likewise, newspapers have largely become geographically specialized. Tichenor and Wackman, for example, have reported the results of a study in metropolitan Minneapolis which clarifies the specialized role of the suburban community newspaper as opposed to the metropolitan paper.[4] Suburban newspapers today are one of the fastest growing areas of the communication industry. Tichenor and Wackman conclude that the function of the community newspaper is to provide cohesion and support for the local community when challenged from outside while the role of the metropolitan paper is to disseminate information between competing interests in the overall social system which contains many communities.

Radio can also be classified with magazines and community newspapers as a highly specialized medium. Honan pointed out that radio has specialized into black radio stations, country—western stations, and several varieties of talk show stations. This variety, he added, has been made possible by fractionalizing the audience and by creating a new "product" for advertisers.

The first two chapters in Part II. document the nature of the trend toward specialized media today. According to Gumpert the media still have large audiences, but these audiences segment according to specialized interests. Maisel, likewise, shows that the demand for specialized media has increased at a faster rate than has the demand for mass media.

In the next chapter of Part II, David Finn adds the specialized newsletter to this list of specialized media. He says specialized newsletters are typified by the spate of energy newsletters which have appeared since the birth of the energy crisis. Finn also examines the implications of the switch to specialization for public relations practitioners who use the media. For example, he says specialization has made the reprint an important public relations tool, because with more media, each individual has less time to spend with each of the media. Therefore, the reprint can bring an article to the busy reader who did not have time to read the specialized publication in which it appeared.

The only true "mass" medium today is television. But, as argued in Chapter 1, it is in the best interests of the television industry to create a mass audience. The audience does not appear to demand a mass medium. According to Melody, it is only when the audience for television would normally be small––such as in the afternoon or on Saturday mornings––and when an advertiser has a number of competitors that the networks find specialized programming more profitable than mass programming. [5]

Because of the economic constraints on commercial television, many media critics look to public television for specialized programming. In the last chapter of this section, Lyle points out that the most popular programs on public television have been cultural programs, special public affairs programs––such as the Watergate hearings–– and quality children's programming. While the audiences for these programs may be small by network standards, three million people still constitute an average audience—— a "mass" audience of specialized interests. Lyle also says that in contrast to commercial television, the Corporation for Public Broadcasting conducts research to develop programs oriented to the interests of audiences and not to the interests of the industry. Although public television may develop as a specialized alternative, he adds, it still would not relieve commercial television of its obligation to present "alternative" programming.

---

1. William H. Honan, "The New Sound of Radio," The *New York Times Magazine*, Dec. 3, 1967, pp. 56–57.

2. Alex S. Edelsten, *The Uses of Communication in Decision Making* (New York: Praeger Special Studies, 1974).

3. Don R. Pember, *Mass Media in America* (Chicago: Science Research Associates, 1974), pp. 334–341.

4. Phillip J. Tichenor and Daniel B. Wackman, "Mass Media and Community Public Opinion," *American Behavioral Scientist* 16 (1973), pp. 593–606.

5. William Melody, *Children's Television: The Economics of Exploitation* (New Haven: Yale University Press, 1973), pp. 11–17.

5

THE RISE OF MINI–COMM

Gary Gumpert

To point out that contemporary society is in the midst of a communication explosion is to state the obvious. Certainly man is bombarded, caressed, fondled, soothed, harangued, influenced, swayed, narcotized, entertained, and taught via the mass media. But the image of the mass communication phenomenon is not quite accurate. The phrase "media of mass communication" does not adequately describe the present media process. The purpose of this discussion is to amend the presently held concept of "mass–comm." In order to achieve this goal it will be necessary to provide a common ground by describing those characteristics which currently define the area of mass communication. Then the concept of "mass–comm" will be related to some of the grand theories of McLuhan, Stephenson, and Loevinger. It is the author's contention that these theories provide only a partial and incomplete explanation of media process and impact. Finally, a modification will be suggested of our current view of mass communication.

The term "mass communication" is a generic one. It is

a shortened form of the phrase "media of mass communication." According to Joseph Klapper, "the term connotes all mass media of communication in which a mechanism of impersonal reproduction intervenes between the speaker and the audience." [1] Therefore, a number of forms can be excluded; theatre, personal conversation, and public address. The following basic characteristics define the mass communication event:

1. Mass communication is public communication.

It is not private communication involving carrier pigeon, secret code, or semaphore signals. The content of mass communication is open to public inspection and is available to that public.

2. The dissemination of mass communication content is rapid.

Rapidity refers to speed in transmission and speed in production. Some media operate with a sense of simultaneity. That is, events will be perceived by a large mass of people at the same time the event is occurring. This generally includes the electronic media. The print media, however, are based upon speed of production rather than simultaneous transmission. The ultimate expression of speed in production is exemplified by the "Instant Book" born with the publication of the *Report of the Warren Commission.* The Instant Book is one based on the coverage of an important government or legal report and is published in a matter of days on a crash schedule. The two main publishers in this area are Bantam and New American Library. Bantam had prepared two covers, ahead of time, for the trial of James Earl Ray—one for guilty and one for innocent. Within about ten days after the conclusion of the trial, *The Strange Case of James Earl Ray* hit the newsstands.

3. The content of mass media is transient.

For the most part, the content or product is meant for consumption on a short—term basis. The products are not meant to endure—unless you are an academic saver of all things. The content is manufactured rather than created. Not all mass communication content can be described as "kitch." There are exceptions, of course, since the techniques of mass communication can be used for the dissemination of enduring ideas and content. We can distinguish between the formula—based paperbacks such as *The Violent Erotics, Sex Secrets of the Mod Wife, Girls Together, Innocent in Chicago,* and *Romance of Lust* and Henry Miller's *The Tropic of Cancer.* The philosophical intent of the communicator must be considered. Generally, however, when the mass audience is sought, content becomes standardized. The typical television situation comedy represents standardized content based upon a formula.

4. The direct cost to the public of mass communication content is minimal.

The indirect costs are very high—the supermarket costs. The mass media are available to most people because of low direct costs. Over 95% of American households own television sets (57 million U. S. households). [2] As of March 20, 1969, there were 6,593 radio stations on the air in this nation. [3]

5. The mass communication audience is large, heteroge—neous, and anonymous.

The audience consists of a great number of isolated

individuals who are not known to each other or by the communicator. A large audience is "any audience exposed for a short time and of such a size that the communicator could not interact with its members on a face–to–face basis". There is, therefore, an obvious lack of immediate feedback which characterizes the mass–comm situation.

6. The nature of the mass communication institution is complex.

The mass communicator, broadly defined, is a corporate organization embodying an extensive division of labor and a high degree of expense. For example, the ABC–20th Century Fox contract for 23 motion pictures involved 20 million dollars. The average half–hour show on CBS costs 94 thousand dollars to produce. The production expenses emphasize the commonplace, since the advertiser deals with a concept or standard of cost per thousand. He seeks the greatest return for his money. At the same time, the pro–duction expenses decrease the access to the media for people who wish to use them.

Mass–comm is represented by the world of the conglom–erate corporation. It is manifested by national sameness. It is often described by the minority as the establishment. It is a one–dimensional view of national culture. In order to exist as the mass media, sameness or oneness is per–petuated in the search for the largest possible audience. The broadcasting rating game is a trap from which there is no escape–if the mass media are to retain their present status. What we have, or more accurately, had, is a monopoly of gatekeepers. There is little difference between a *Life* magazine or a *Look* magazine. Nor is there a significant difference between CBS and NBC or between the Hollywood films produced by Columbia and those produced by Paramount. In fact, the relationship between Hollywood and the television networks represents another dimension of actual or contractual conglomerate corporations and the monopoly of ideas.

It is this milieu of mass—comm that is dealt with by the grand theorists. William Stephenson's "Play Theory of Mass Communication" might also be called the "Sham Theory of Mass Communication." The crux of Stephenson's theory is that people consume most mass communication because they derive pleasure and subjective fulfillment from it. He dismisses the common cry of media manipulation of the masses, and he claims that because the individual has an extremely broad choice of programming (or reading material, etc.), selecting that which best suits his needs, the individual is subjectively manipulating the mass media. Stephenson calls this subjective free choice, "convergent selectivity," and claims it is a new development in history, a by—product of the mass media which permits a "heightened self-awareness". [4] This individuality of choice is quite desirable for it permits us "to exist for ourselves, to please ourselves, free to a degree from social control". [5] But the "communication pleasure" of which Stephenson speaks is an illusion through which an individual is kept busy via the provision of the daily "fill" by the media of mass communication. Stephenson presents an elitist theory and thereby provides a rationale for the existence of mass—comm. It is ironic that he preaches the selectivity of sham, because the reality of selectivity is evident in the newer developments of mini-comm.

Lee Loevinger's "Reflective–Projective Theory of Broadcasting and Mass Communication"..."postulating that mass communications are best understood as mirrors of society that reflect an ambiguous image in which each observer projects or sees his own vision of himself and society",[6] is an apology in the guise of an explanation for the nature of American broadcasting. The most provocative aspect of Loevinger's theory is his belief that in the field of communications, media technology reverses psychology in order of development. Loevinger provides a challenge to the McLuhan "Hot–Cool" media syndrome.

Television is a medium which...conveys the most information in the most literal form by giving us oral language combined with visual perceptions and requiring the least effort to interpret the abstractions. Thus television is a multichannel communication which is more elemental and therefore has greater immediacy and impact than other media.[7]

The Reflective–Projective theory deals with an explanation of the mass impact of the mass media of communication–of media which seem to reach the greatest possible share of an available audience. But what about WEVD in New York City which at one time was advertising for a Chinese disc jockey? "Applicants must be acquainted with Poon Sow Keng (the hottest rock 'n' roll singer today in Hong Kong), be able to report the time, news and temperature in easy going Cantonese, and quote Confucius in the original".[8] What about the *National Turkey News, The New York Review of Books,* underground films, or television for stock–brokers? Where do they belong?

It is difficult to evaluate the theory of Marshall McLuhan, if there is one theory. During some correspondence McLuhan clarified his point of view.

My theme is quite simple, in this respect at least; that I see the entire Gutenberg 500 years as a repetition in all levels of life and culture of the basic matrix of the Gutenberg press itself. The Greeko—Roman world, from the phonetic alphabet forward, was in the same way a repetition of the technology of that alphabet as applied to papyrus and to—day our world shows the beginnings of a repetition in all human transactions of the basic electric circuit. I mention this because if we can consider the 500 years of Gutenberg dominance as located between two other technologies, it should help to define our problems. [9]

There have been few effective critics of McLuhan. Most of them capitulate by attacking his style. McLuhan should be considered a Happening—a most effective Happening, since his message appears to equally effect and explain the nature of media. Man began in the tribal village. The media have accelerated the process of returning him to a tribal existence—the tribal world.

Through radio, TV, and the computer, we are already entering a global theatre in which the entire world is a Happening...a simultaneous "all—at—one" world in which everything resonates with everything else as in a total electrical field... [10]

We have all experienced a taste of this global village. For some people the tribal world is rather disturbing and threatening. McLuhan speaks of the United States "as a nation which is doomed, in any case, to break up into a series of regional and racial ministates". [11] Obviously, man can communicate with any part of the world if world politics allows him the freedom of his capability. Media do not have to heed the warning of national boundaries. But what happens to the needs of primary groups, subgroups, and specific communities or cultures in that global village? It seems that Marshall McLuhan does not provide a satisfactory answer to that question. He speaks of "the electronically induced technological extensions of our central nervous system", [12] but he does not account for the communication vacuums induced by global interrelationships and a situation in which communication channels are monopolized by the few.

It is Harold A. Innis in *The Basis of Communication* who provides an explanation of the process which has created the need for a shift or modification of our current thinking in regard to mass communication. In his scholarly fashion, he shows that a monopoly of knowledge creates new media in the way that the "monopoly of knowledge centering around stone and hieroglyphics was exposed to competition from papyrus as a new and more efficient medium". [13] He suggests that "a stable society is dependent on an appreciation of a proper balance between the concepts of space and time". [14] The key word is balance. Although stability of a civilization is rarely achieved, it can occur only when competitive balance and a non-monopolistic climate prevail. Innis can be interpreted to say that when monopoly of knowledge prevails, this very situation stimulates the need and invention of countering media. And this is what is happening today and will continue to happen.

The "traditional" concept of mass communications no longer describes "the way it really is." There is a psycho-sociological want for media which are addressed to us, our own group—as we see ourselves as members of a society. As isolated entities in a mass society individuals wish to be heard, to be linked with others like themselves. This coupling is manifested in geographical or avocational binding. At times, the focus is on the immediate community. At other times, the focus is upon a belief system which transcends geographical lines. This focusing is accomplished through media of communication which reach specific select audiences, and yet these audiences consist of enough people to fit the criteria of a mass audience. They are, however, a small mass audience. In addition, this audience is motivated to non-standardized content. The author refers to this development as the rise of "mini-comm." Mass-comm still exists and serves important functions, but it is a coexistence and not sole-existence.

A cursory examination of several media will indicate the trend toward mini-comm.

1. Magazines

For many people the death of the *Saturday Evening Post* suggested the final demise of the magazine field. The opposite is true. In 1968, ninety-four new magazines were started, nine others merged or were sold, and only twelve went out of business. According to John Tebbel, writing in the *Saturday Review*:

65

In a country of two hundred million people, producing successful mass magazines has become increasingly more difficult, while those reaching smaller audiences within the mass have been increasingly successful. Thirty years ago a magazine with a circulation of 500,000 to 3,000,000 was considered large, or even mass, and most specialized publications were limping along with circulations ranging roughly from 50,000 to 150,000. Today a magazine has to have more than 6,000,000 to play with the big boys.[15]

The magazine world is adopting new methods and is carefully analyzing its markets. Some publications are based upon controlled circulation methods—they are sent free to more or less carefully selected audiences. *Charlie* is a magazine for coeds under twenty—five and is mailed to department store customers. Started in 1968, *Charlie* is expected to have a circulation between 150,000 and 200,000. *Go* is a free circulation tabloid distributed through record stores in thirty—five cities with a 750,000 circulation. Magazines are published in the name of cities and states— *New York Magazine, Florida, The New Californian,* and *Arizona Highways.* There is a publication for everyone. Among the limitless list can be found *Afternoon TV, Censorship Today, Modern Bride's Guide to Decorating Your First Home, Yellow Submarine, Government Photography, Musical Electronics, Weight Watchers,* and the *Southern Hog Producer.* The left and right of the political spectrum, and shades in between, have publications which link the be— lievers. Part of a more serious list includes *Ramparts, Saturday Review, America, Atlantic Monthly, Harpers,* and the *Reporter.* These are publications which probably affect

66

the decision—making process in our society. Are they exam—
ples of mass communication?

2. Radio

The FM spectrum is now fractionalized, and the AM
spectrum is becoming fractionalized. In New York, and that
city is unique only in terms of numbers, there is a left—of—
center, a high—brow good music, a low—brow good music,
and all—ethnic stations have been around for some time. The
manager of one noncommercial FM station, WRVR, stated
that a recent survey revealed 32% of that station's audience
had some postgraduate education. In New York, suburban
radio consists of twenty—nine AM and fifteen FM stations.
You listen to suburban radio to find out whether the schools
are open, which ice ponds are safe, the score of the local
basketball game, and the scandal of the week. WNBC and
WCBS serve the New York megalopolis. But do they serve
the unique pockets of community that exist both within and
outside large urban areas? "Henry S. Hovland, general
manager of WGCH in Greenwich, thinks the success of his
and other suburban stations is not service or even snobbery,
but 'seeking an identity in megalopolis, not for the stations,
for the people; they resent being swallowed up' ". [16] Mini—
comm provides a partial answer to an individual's quest for
identity and the individual has the added advantage of
changing that identity with the mini—comm he chooses.

3. Television

In the near future it will be possible for each home to have thirty channels available. The rise of UHF, Public Television, and most important, CATV tends to support the contention that the medium will become fractionalized. In addition, satellite communication has the potential of altering the present configuration of television transmission. The days of the network might be doomed.

4. Newspapers

The daily newspaper is on the decline, but the weekly is rising in importance and number. The *New York Times* does not adequately serve the typical suburban community. The ordinary traffic accident involving one or two deaths is often not reported in the *New York Times*. A local paper is required for that piece of information. In fact, a number of papers and media is necessary in order for the individual to understand the operation and nature of his environment. Jack Lyle in *The News in Megalopolis* makes the point that:

While the specialty press may not be able (or even wish) to vie with the daily press in performing the general function of maintaining a general surveillance of the environment, they do compete with the daily press in attempting to correlate society's interpretation of, and reaction to, the major events of the period. [17]

In this way, mini–comm supplements mass–comm.

In addition to community papers, the underground papers (not really a satisfactory label) continue to grow in circulation and importance. When the *Village Voice* veered from its avant–garde position, a number of other papers filled the void: *Other Scenes, Rolling Stone, The New York Review of Sex, Rat, Fun, Screw, Jive Comics,* and *The East Village Other.* Such papers are not limited to New York. Sold on the newsstand and by subscription, their existence cannot be dismissed. What are the functions of *The Berkeley Barb,* the *Los Angeles Free Press,* and *The Black Panther?* The papers continue to proliferate and some are united through the service of an underground news service.

The same trends can be found in the motion picture area, the recording industry, and the comic book field. The causal relationships of mini–comm and mass–comm are demonstrated by the developments in each medium. While mini-comm fills needs not served by mass–comm, both tend to define each other and influence each other.

The Hollywood film helped to create the independent producer who, in turn, influenced the birth of the art film. The underground film is also a response and has influenced the total film industry. The "new" film has had a fantastic impact. Part of this impact is described by Anthony Schillaci when he discussed "Film as Environment" in the *Saturday Review:*

The new multisensory involvement with film as total environment has been primary in destroying literary values in film...it means the emergence of a new identity for film. [18]

69

The recording field is an exciting kingdom of creativity which caters to a stratified audience. The Jefferson Airplane's "White Rabbit" is aimed at an acid sympathetic subgroup. Tim Buckley's "No Man Can Find the War" is an anti-Vietnam statement. There is a grammar of "rock" which the older generation refuses to learn.

The comic book is another example of splendid splinters. How do you generalize about "Young Romance," "Superman," and "The Silver Surfer" (a comic book you must read in order to believe)? "Feiffer," "B. C.," "Pogo," "Peanuts," "Dick Tracy," "Lil Abner," and "Little Orphan Annie" are comic strips which accurately reflect the problems and philosophies of our society. They appeal to sections of the mass, not necessarily to the entire mass.

The rise of mini-comm is going to require some adjustments on the part of the academic community. There is a need for research which examines mini-comm. Since mini-communication alters the functions of mass-comm, a new functional analysis of media is in order. It is time to reexamine the "Two Step Flow of Communication"—in light of newer configurations of primary groups and subgroups. Content analysis would also be highly revealing.

In addition to research, it is most important that man learn to cope with a multiplicity of sounds and images. He may think that he is bombarded now, but the barrage is going to increase. And the increase will bring with it the individual and his wisdom. It will take wisdom and perception to tolerate and perhaps understand the alien, the strange, and the opposition. Diversity brings with it the multiple point of view and the proclivity to condemn the opposition and the ideology of commitment. To condemn the right of man to express himself is to censor in the name of a creed in vogue. The result is merely to drive ideas underground, for ideas can never be destroyed. Mini–comm will play a critical role in the future, if it is allowed to thrive.

---

1.   George Gerbner. "Mass Media and Human Communication Theory." In *Human Communication Theory.* (Edited by Frank E. X. Dance.) New York: Holt, Rinehart and Winston, 1967, p. 44.

2.   *Nielsen Television 1969,* Chicago: A. C. Nielsen, 1969, p. 5.

3.   "Summary of Broadcasting." *Broadcasting 76:* 168, March 24, 1969.

3A.   Charles R. Wright. *Mass Communication: A Sociological Perspective.* New York: Random House, 1964, p. 13.

4.   William Stephenson. *The Play Theory of Mass Communication.* Chicago: University of Chicago Press, 1967, p. 35.

5.   *Ibid.,* p. 2.

6.   Lee Loevinger. "The Ambiguous Mirror: The Reflective–Projective Theory of Broadcasting and Mass Communications." *Journal of Broadcasting* 12:108, Spring 1968.

7.   *Ibid.,* p. 110.

8.   William H. Honan. "The New Sound of Radio." *The New York Times Magazine,* December 3, 1967, p.56.

9.   Letter from Marshall McLuhan, May 5, 1960.

10.   "Playboy Interview: Marshall Mc Luhan." *Playboy*, March 1969, p. 70.

11.   *Ibid.*

12.   *Ibid.*, p. 62.

13.   Harold A. Innis. *The Bias of Communication*. Toronto: University of Toronto Press, 1951, p. 35.

14.   *Ibid.*, p. 64.

15.   John Tebbel. "Magazines—New, Changing, Growing." *Saturday Review*, February 8, 1969, p. 55.

16.   Robert Windeler. "Radio and Suburbs Discover Each Other," *New York Times*, December 30, 1968, p. 24.

17.   Jack Lyle. *The News in Megalopolis*. San Francisco: Chandler, 1967, p. 36–37.

18.   Anthony Schillaci. "The New Movie: 1. Film as Environment." *Saturday Review*, December 28, 1968, p. 9.

6

THE DECLINE OF MASS MEDIA*

Richard Maisel

A new, three–stage theory of social change and media–growth, formulated in recent years, challenges many of the ideas long accepted in the study of modern communications systems. According to this theory, the third stage, now evident in the United States, is characterized by a declining growth rate for mass media and an increasing growth rate for specialized communication directed to smaller, more homogeneous audiences.[1] If this theory is correct, the mass media will—contrary to past expectations—play a less important role in the future, and the focus of scientific attention should be shifted to specialized media.

This article reviews media growth trends in the United States during the period 1950–70[2] to determine whether the claims of the three–stage theory are warranted.

THE TWO–STAGE THEORY[3]

Most studies of modern communications systems are based on a two–stage theory of social change and media growth, which may be summarized as follows:

1. The history of Western civilization may meaningfully be divided into two periods: a stable earlier period, in which society was small in scale, local in orientation, and organized around a primitive, pre–industrial economy; and a later period of industrialization, extending to the present, in which society has grown in size, scope, and technological prowess.

2. Each of these two periods is characterized by a communication system that is consistent with its needs and resources. In the pre–industrial period, the communication system was restricted to direct face–to–face communication between individuals. In the later period, beginning in the mid–fifteenth century with the invention of printing from movable type, a powerful system of mass communication evolved.

3. There is a close, functional relationship between the process of industrialization and the growth of mass communication. The former stimulates and provides the resources necessary for the latter; the latter facilitates the growth of the former. Thus each stage in the growth of the mass media helps provide the conditions necessary for its further growth.

4. Both the mass media and the processes of industrialization that support it have been growing at a rapid rate and will continue to do so in the future.

5. Mass communication develops a powerful "hold" over its audience, thereby closing off potentially competitive forms of cultural experience. This gives the mass media an ever more secure position and an ever more paramount role in determining the cultural content of our society.

74

THE THREE–STAGE THEORY[4]

The newer, three–stage theory of social change and media growth incorporates the older theory through step 3, supplanting the later steps with a third stage of development, as follows:

4. When industrialization and the institutional changes that accompany it reach an advanced level, new forces are released, which channel subsequent social and economic development down a new path, culminating in the third stage–"post–industrial society."

5. Among the forces released at an advanced level of industrialization are increased specialization and the growth of the so–called service industries.

6. The point at which the third stage begins is usually marked by a rapid shift of the work force away from the manufacturing sector toward the service sector. In the United States, this shift occurred in the period following the second World War.

7. The service industries are great consumers of spec–ialized media. The needs and tastes of specialized groups can only be satisfied by a form of specialized communication designed for homogeneous audiences.

Thus, the development of the third stage, or "post–industrial society," does not support the rapid growth of mass communication; rather, it stimulates the growth of specialized media. Moreover, technological development and increase in wealth provide the means necessary for the development of these specialized media.

On the basis of these propositions, we would not predict an acceleration in the growth of the mass media; rather, we

75

would expect a rapid growth in specialized media.

TEST OF HYPOTHESIS

According to the three—stage theory, the United States entered the third stage following the second World War. Therefore, we may test the theory by examining the rates of media growth in the United States during the period 1950–70, expecting to find an increase in growth rates for the specialized media relative to growth rates for the mass media. We shall measure the growth of media in two ways. First, we shall measure economic support, in current dollars,[5] including advertising revenue, consumer expenditures, and, in some cases, government expenditures. Second, we shall measure growth in the volume of communications using the best measures available throughout the period.[6]

MASS MEDIA, EDUCATION, AND PERSONAL MESSAGE SYSTEM

The education system is the most important of all specialized media systems. At its core is the school system, a mammoth medium for the communication of specialized information. The school system also supports the use of other specialized media, such as textbooks, technical treatises, and audio—visual materials. Equally important, the product of the education system, particularly of *higher* education, is a stratum of individuals who, both in their work and private life, are consumers of specialized communication. Thus, a crucial test of the three—stage theory is provided by growth in the education system.

76

In this section, we will compare the growth rates for the education system with those of the mass media. To complete the analysis, we will include the growth rates of the much–neglected personal message system, which includes those specialized media, other than face–to–face interaction, that permit communication between individuals. These include the telephone, telegraph, and correspondence by mail. If the three–stage theory is correct, we should expect to find that the growth rates for both the education and personal message systems are greater than those for the mass media. Analysis of education growth rates, however, remains the more crucial test.

Table 1, depicting economic growth for the mass media,

TABLE 1

VOLUME AND GROWTH RATE OF GNP, EDUCATION, PERSONAL MESSAGE, AND MASS MEDIA SYSTEMS, 1950–70

| GNP and Media | Dollar Volume (GNP in Billions, Media Systems in Millions) | | | Growth Rate | |
	1950	1960	1970	1950–60	1960–70
GNP[a]	284.8	503.7	974.1	1.78	1.93
Media Systems					
Education[b]	8,796	24,722	70,600	2.81	2.85
Personal Message[c]	4,544	10,001	20,636	2.20	2.06
Mass Media[d]	9,254	16,413	28,525	1.77	1.73

[a] *Abstract 1971,* Table 150.
[b] Consists of educational expenditure at all levels of instruction, public and private (*Abstract 1972,* Table 155).
[c] Consists of telephone and telegraph operating revenue, domestic and overseas (*Abstract 1972,* Table 793) and ordinary postal revenue (*Abstract 1971,* Table 752).
[d] Consists of advertising revenue (*Abstract 1972,* Table 1260), consumer expenditure on books, maps, newspapers, magazines, sheet music, and motion pictures (*Abstract 1972,* Table 330), and the number of subscribers to CATV (*Abstract 1972,* Table 802) times an assumed annual subscription rate of $50.

education, and personal message systems, reveals the highest growth rate in the education system, and the lowest growth rate in the mass media system. Table 1 also shows growth rates for the economy as a whole measured as the gross national product (GNP). The growth rates for both the education and personal message systems are well above those for the GNP, indicating that both of these systems— but particularly education—expanded relative to the total economy. The growth rate for the mass media was approx- imately equal to that of the GNP in the 1950–60 period, but fell behind during the 1960–70 period. Thus, we must con- clude that the mass media system is contracting relative to the economy as a whole.

Every media system is composed of new and expanding segments, as well as those that are stable or in decline. The critical element in the development of media systems is found in the growth segments. Table 2 shows the growth rates, measured in terms of dollar–value and facility use, for television, the telephone, and higher education—the most active components of, respectively, the mass media, personal message, and education systems. As we would expect, Table 2 reveals explosive growth for television during the 1950–55 period, but a steady decline in its expansion thereafter. In contrast, the growth rate for higher education was low in the 1950–55 period, but rose sharply in subsequent periods. By the 1955–60 period, the growth rate for higher education had surpassed that of television, and continued to do so throughout the sixties. The growth rate for the telephone was moderately high compared to the other two media under consideration, and stable through–

TABLE 2
GROWTH RATE OF HIGHER EDUCATION, TELEPHONE,
AND TELEVISION, 1950–70

Media	Growth Rate			
	1950–55	1955–60	1960–65	1965–70
Dollar Volume				
Higher Education[a]	1.52	2.05	1.94	1.93
Telephone[b]	1.70	1.43	1.41	1.52
Television[c]	6.04	1.57	1.59	1.44
Communication Volume				
Higher Education[d]	1.07	1.50	1.58	1.30
Telephone[e]	1.22	1.33	1.29	1.33
Television[f]	4.38	1.46	1.30	1.19

[a] Current expenditure and interest, capital outlay, or plant expansion (*Abstract 1971*, Table 150), except 1955 data, which were estimated by assuming 1955 expenditure to be equal to 1950 expenditure plus five–sixths of the growth to 1956 (*Abstract 1972*, Table 139).

[b] Operating revenue, domestic and overseas (*Abstract 1971*, Table 759) except 1955 data (*Abstract 1960*, Table 663).

[c] Advertising revenue (*Abstract 1972*, Table 1216) and the number of subscribers to CATV (*Abstract 1972*, Table 802) times an assumed annual subscription rate of $50.

[d] College enrollment *Abstract 1971*, Table 153).

[e] Average telephone conversations daily, Bell and independent companies, local and long distance (*Abstract 1971* Table 757), except 1955 data (*Abstract 1960*, Table 665).

[f] Average total hours sets in use daily, obtained by the number of television households (A. C. Nielson Company, *Television 1971*, p. 5) times the average hours per day of television sets in use per household (National Association of Broadcasters, *Dimensions of Television 1968–69*, p. 12 and 'A. C. Nielson Company, private communication).

79

out the postwar period. In the 1965–70 period, it surpassed the sagging growth rate for television. Thus, in the 1950–70 period, growth rates for the fastest growing segments of the education and personal message systems have increased relative to the analogous component of the mass media system. Moreover, television dollar volume grew by 1.44 during the 1965–70 period, insignificantly more than the 1.43 by which the GNP grew in the same interval. Therefore, by 1970, television, which is usually considered the most successful of the mass media, did not have an expanding position in the economy.

Each medium may also be divided into more or less specialized segments. Higher education, for example, tends to be a more specialized medium, while elementary school tends to be a mass medium. Thus we can test the three-stage theory by examining the growth rates for each medium divided into segments along degree–of–specialization lines. In the case of the school system, expenditures in the 1960–70 period grew by 1.14 for elementary schools, 1.43 for secondary schools, and 2.07 for institutions of higher education. Thus growth rates vary directly with the degree of specialization of the individual segment. The same general tendencies are seen in Table 3, which shows that the growth rates for education and special service broadcasting have been increasing relative to those of commercial broadcasting. Table 4 shows that in the 1960–70 period, the quantity of air and first–class mail delivered increased faster than second, third and fourth–class mail (excluding publications), and the purchase rate of tape recorders exceeded that of phonographs.

TABLE 3

GROWTH RATE OF COMMERCIAL, EDUCATIONAL, AND SPECIAL SERVICE
BROADCASTING, 1950–70

	Growth Rate			
	1950–55	*1955–60*	*1960–65*	*1965–70*
Number of Authorized Radio Stations				
Educational[a]	1.58	1.42	1.50	1.69
Safety and Special Service[b]	1.24	2.17	2.23	1.26
Commercial[c]	1.10	1.31	1.27	1.17
Number of TV Stations on Air[d]				
Educational	—	4.27	1.95	2.06
Commercial	4.40	1.25	1.01	1.15
Average Weekly Hours of Broadcasting per TV Station				
Educational[e]	—	—	—	1.42
Commercial[f]	—	—	—	1.02

[a]FM only (*Abstract 1966,* Table 737), except 1970 data
(*Abstract 1971,* Table 765).

[b]Consists of amateur, disaster, citizens, aviation, industrial
industrial, marine, land transportation, and public safety devices
(*Abstract 1971,* Table 765).

[c]AM and FM (*Abstract 1966,* Table 737), except 1970 data
(*Abstract 1971,* Table 765).

[d]Federal Communications Commission, *Annual Report, Fiscal
Year 1970,* p. 144.

[e]*Abstract 1972,* Table 803. Data for 1965 were estimated as
the average of 1964 and 1966 data.

[f]*Abstract 1972,* Table 809.

81

TABLE 4

VOLUME AND GROWTH RATE OF MAIL AND CONSUMER AUDIO EQUIPMENT,

1950–70

	Unit Volume			Growth Rate	
	1950	1960	1970	1950–60	1960–70
Mail Received,[a] Pieces per Capita					
Air and First-class	168	193	246	1.14	1.27
Second-, Third-, and Fourth-class	119	148	149	1.24	1.01
Consumer Audio Equipment,[b] in Thousands of Units Purchased					
Tape Recorders	—	295	8,452	—	28.65
Phonographs	1,260	4,523	5,620	3.58	1.24

[a] *Abstract 1971,* Table 752.
[b] Electronic Industry Association, *Consumer Electronics 1972.*

Therefore, every comparison among the education, personal message, and mass media systems shows that the first two media are growing at increasingly more rapid rates than the third.

SPECIALIZATION OF THE MASS MEDIA

Several authors[8] have suggested that the mass media themselves are becoming more specialized, a proposition deduced from the three–stage theory. We can test this proposition by examining the growth rates of the more specialized and less specialized components of each mass medium. We can, for example, distinguish between the national broadcasting networks and local radio and television stations; the former have larger and more heterogeneous audiences and thereby constitute the less specialized segment of the broadcasting media. Table 5 shows that within all three of the major media—radio, newspapers, and magazines—throughout the years 1950 to 1970 there has been greater growth in advertising revenue directed to more specialized audiences. This finding strongly supports the three—stage theory in two ways: (1) by showing differential growth in the media carrying the advertising, and (2) by *directly* showing differential growth in the medium of advertising, itself a means of communication. The source of support also suggests the direction to which the media must orient themselves in order to obtain further support: the growth of a more specialized type of advertising means the medium must attract the type of audience to which a more specialized advertising is directed. Thus, specialized advertising becomes a factor in the medium's continued specialization. An outstanding example of this can be seen in the case of radio, where network—originated broadcasts have diminished in favor of locally based fare directed to very special segments within the community. Thus, one station will play "heavy" rock music, while another station operates in the older "top 40" rock 'n' roll format, and a third broadcasts news exclusively. The trend has gone so far that the newtorlw, themselves, have become specialized. The same trend can be found in the area of magazines, in which mass magazines such as *Life, Look,* and the *Saturday Evening Post* have ceased publication, while

83

TABLE 5

GROWTH RATE OF GNP AND ADVERTISING EXPENDITURE BY MEDIUM,
1950–69

	Growth Rate			
GNP and Media	1950–55	1955–60	1960–65	1965–69
GNP[a]	1.40	1.26	1.36	1.35
Television[b]				
Network	6.35	1.45	1.57	1.35
Local	4.09	1.24	1.46	1.58
Radio[c]				
Network	.43	.51	1.39	.98
Local	1.19	1.31	1.37	1.42
Magazine				
Regional[d]	—	—	2.06	1.35
Other than Regional[e]	1.41	1.29	1.20	1.11
Newspaper[f]				
National	1.39	1.13	1.03	1.20
Retail	1.48	1.18	1.14	1.28
Classified	1.61	1.31	1.51	1.30
All Media[g]				
National	1.66	1.35	1.28	1.22
Local	1.54	1.22	1.27	1.35
Total	1.61	1.29	1.27	1.28

[a] *Abstract 1971*, Table 484.

[b] *Abstract 1971*, Table 1216.

[c] *Ibid.*

[d] Publishers' Information Bureau/Leading National Advertisers.

[e] Total magazine advertising expenditure (*Abstract 1971*,
Table 1216) minus regional advertising expenditure, *ut supra*.

[f] American Newspaper Publishers Association, Research
Department, Bureau of Advertising, March 1970.

[g] *Abstract 1971*, Table 1216.

special interest magazines have been thriving. Many maga—zines with large national circulations, such as *Time,* have set up regional advertising areas.

The trend toward specialization in magazines and radio has often been noted before,[9] and is usually explained as a consequence of television. But this is only a partial explanation. It does not, for example, explain the fact that the growth rate of local television advertising has been increasing relative to the growth rate for network television advertising (Table 5). The three—stage theory accounts not only for shifts among media, but for shifts within a particular medium as well.

In Table 6, data for the 1950–70 period reveal that the growth rate of consumer economic support for various media is directly related to the degree in which each medium is specialized. Within the print medium, the growth rate for books has been higher than for magazines and newspapers, which are less specialized, and the rate of increase in expenditures for legitimate theater has been greater than than the rate of increase in expenditures for motion pictures, which again are less specialized. Table 6 also shows that the rate of increase in consumer expenditures for radio, television, magazines, newspapers and motion pictures has been far less than the rate of increase in consumer expenditure as a whole, which in turn has been less than the rate of increase in books and legitimate theater. This further confirms that, relative to the total economy, spe—cialized media are expanding and mass media are contract—ing.

Table 7, providing 1947–70 growth rates for various

TABLE 6

1950–70

Medium	Growth Rate			
	1950–55	1955–60	1960–65	1965–70
Radio and Television[a]	1.25	1.25	1.67	1.40
Magazines and Newspapers[b]	1.25	1.17	1.30	1.42
Books[c]	1.29	1.50	1.54	1.66
Legitimate Theater[d]	1.34	1.48	1.35	1.48
Motion Pictures[e]	1.01	.89	1.12	1.33
Total[f]	1.26	1.29	1.43	1.48

[a]Consists of expenditure for purchase and repair of radio and television receivers, phonograph records and musical instruments (*Abstract 1972*, Table 330), and the number of subscribers to CATV (*Abstract 1972*, Table 802) times an assumed annual subscription rate of $50.

[b]*Abstract 1972*, Table 330. Includes sheet music.

[c]*Abstract 1972*, Table 330. Includes maps.

[d]*Abstract 1972*, Table 330.

[e]*Ibid.*

[f]*Ibid.*

segments within the print medium, reveals that in every case, growth of the more specialized segment of the medium exceeds that of the less specialized; the growth rate in the circulation of suburban newspapers is greater than the growth rate in the circulation of central city newspapers; the growth rate in the number of technical books sold and the number of new technical books published is greater than the growth rate in the number of fiction books sold

DECLINE OF MASS MEDIA

TABLE 7

VOLUME AND GROWTH RATE OF PRINT MEDIA, 1947-70

Print Media	Unit Volume			Growth Rate	
	1947	1957	1967	1947-57	1957-67
Newspaper Circulation, 25 Largest Metropolitan Areas,[a] in Millions of Papers Sold					
Central City Papers[b]	22.7	24.7	23.0	1.09	.93
Papers Outside Central City	1.4	2.4	3.5	1.71	1.45
Books,[c] in Millions of Copies Sold					
Fiction[d]	—	480.0	759.2	—	1.58
Technical[e]	—	238.6	602.4	—	1.77
	1950	1960	1970	1950-60	1960-70
New Books and Editions Published[f]					
Fiction	1,907	2,440	3,137	1.28	1.28
Technical[g]	3,200	4,415	13,834	1.37	3.13
Periodicals Published[h]	5,553	6,220	6,759	1.12	1.08
Weekly to Monthly					
Bimonthly and Quarterly	1,040	1,638	2,065	1.56	1.26

[a]M. Lehr and J. Wallis, interoffice correspondence, American Newspaper Publishers Association, Bureau of Advertising, May 3, 1967.

[b]Includes circulation that these papers have outside central city.

[c]*Abstract 1972*, Table 818. Data for 1957 were estimated from 1958 and 1967 data assuming a constant growth rate between 1957 and 1967.

[d]Includes general book, trade, etc.

[e]Includes textbooks, subscription reference books, technical, scientific, and professional books.

[f]*Abstract 1972*, Table 816.

[g]Includes agriculture, business, law, medicine, philosophy, psychology, science, sociology, economics, and technologies.

[h]*Abstract 1972*, Table 810.

and the number of new fiction books published; the growth rate in the number of bimonthly and quarterly magazines is greater than the growth rate in the number of weekly and monthly magazines.

The same trend toward specialization can be seen in the theater medium, where the number of off—Broadway performances increased by 1.29 from 1960–1970, while in the same period the growth rate for the less specialized Broadway performance was .75.[10] An identical trend can be seen in motion pictures, where the size of newly built theaters and their audiences have decreased.

CONCLUSION

Our review of trends in media growth in the United States during the 1950–70 period supports the three—stage theory of social change and media growth. In every case, the growth rate of the more specialized media increased relative to the growth rate of the mass media. The mass media are actually shrinking in size relative to the total economy.

Given these findings, it is clear that the focus of attention in the study of modern communications systems should broaden from its present preoccupation with the mass media to a full examination of all major media and communication systems. This would include studies of important media systems that have been almost completely neglected, such as the telephone system; studies of new media that are growing rapidly, such as the office communications system; and studies that provide perspectives on the total communication system of our society, such as those of   Fritz

Machlup.[11]

We must also abandon the outmoded view of the individual as simply the recipient of standardized messages emanating from the mass media, whose only recourse in self—expression is the primitive sound of his own voice in direct face—to-face interaction. Rather, we must begin to think of, and study the individual in our society as a communicator having access to a very powerful set of media tools and as a recipient of a wide range of equally enriched communications directed to him by others. This would lead us to study how he learns about and uses the available media systems, and the effect that this ability to communicate has on him.

Comparing the two— and three—stage theories shows that it is dangerous simply to project trends into the future. Each development seems to bring with it the conditions by which it changes. Thus the development of the stan—dardized industrial culture brought about the conditions that now seem to be causing the development of a more differentiated culture. We should, therefore, not make the same error of simply projecting the third stage into the the future. At least two other possibilities exist. First, the explosive increase in the volume of communication directed to the individual creates the problem of dealing with it. Thus we might expect the coming period to be characterized by the growth of receptors, media for re—ceiving communications; such developments are already apparent in the use of speed reading, computers for data retrieval, tape recorders, and copying equipment.

The second possibility is less auspicious. The growth of a differentiated communication system is part of the

89

larger process by which our society has been producing a differentiated culture. Both in economic and psychological terms, the cost of this differentiated culture has been increasing, and it is not clear whether our society will pay the price of supporting it in the future. In recent years, for example, both economic and moral support has been withdrawn from educational institutions, which in the past played a leading role in the development of the differentiated culture.

*An earlier version of this paper, "Mass Media: Fact and Fantasy," was presented at the 1966 annual meeting of the American Association for Public Opinion Research. The author wishes to express his thanks to Alan Bell for editorial assistance.

[1]Conversely, we shall assume that larger audiences are more heterogeneous. Here, "audience" means that *average* audience to which messages sent by a particular medium are directed. We acknowledge, but consider it the exception, that larger audiences are sometimes *less* heterogeneous.

[2]Unless otherwise stated, all sources of data given in this article are: U.S. Department of Commerce, Bureau of the Census, *Statistical Abstract of the United States*, Washington D.C., Government Printing Office, 1960–72. This work will hereafter be referred to as *Abstract*, followed by the year of publication and table number.

[3]The two–stage theory was implicitly assumed by both sides several years ago in the then prevalent controversy over mass culture. It is also assumed by several authors as a grounding rationale. See, e.g., Charles S. Steinberg, ed., *Mass Media and Communication*, New York, Hastings House, 1966, pp. ix–xiii; and Lewis Anthony Dexter and David Manning White, eds., *People and Mass Communications*, New York, Free Press, 1964, pp. 3–10. Explicit statements of the two–stage theory may be found in Joseph Bensman and Bernard Rosenberg, "Mass Media and Mass Culture," in Phillip Olsen, ed., *America as a Mass Society*, New York, Free Press, 1963; and Melvin DeFleur, *Theories of Mass Communication*, 2d ed., New York, David McKay, 1970, chs.1–4 and 6.

[4]The three—stage theory is part of a more general shift from two— to three—stage theories of social change. Colin Clark (*Conditions of Economic Progress*, London, MacMillan, 1957) has formulated a widely used three—stage theory of economic growth that has been extended to other areas of society by Daniel Bell ("The Measurement of Knowledge and Technology," in Eleanor Bernert Sheldon and Wilbert E. Moore, eds., *Indicators of Social Change*, New York, Russell Sage, 1968) and others as the post—industrial society." The clearest statement of the three—stage theory as it applies to media growth, and the one used as the basis for this paper, is given by John Merrill and Ralph L. Lowenstein, *Media, Message, and Man*, New York, David McKay, 1971, pp. 33—44.

[5] Since we are interested in relative growth, there is no need to correct for inflation using constant dollars.

[6] In most cases, measures for volume are far from ideal. For example, our measure for the volume of communication by books, the number of books sold, does not take into account the degree to which the books were actually read.

[7] *Abstract 1971*, Table 153.

[8] Merrill and Lowenstein, *op cit.*, pp. 33—44; and Dennis McQuail, *Toward the Sociology of Mass Communication*, London, Collier—MacMillan Ltd., 1969.

[9] See, e.g., Rolf B. Meyerson, "Social Research in Television," in Bernard Rosenberg and David Manning White, eds., *Mass Culture*, New York, Free Press, 1957, pp. 348—49; and Sydney W. Head, "Some Intermedia Relationships," in Steinberg, *op. cit.*

[10] *Abstract 1971*, Table 319.

[11] Fritz Machlup, *The Production and Distribution of Knowledge*, Princeton, N.J., Princeton University Press, 1962.

92

7

THE FUTURE OF SPECIALIZED MEDIA
IN PUBLIC RELATIONS

David Finn

The future is always difficult to anticipate in any field, at least for the non—futurist, and I do not feel I can assert with any great confidence what impact specialized media will have on public relations in the year ahead. One of the most puzzling aspects of the inquiry is that some changes now taking place in the media are having very little effect on public relations, and yet just a few years ago many of us might have predicted very different consequences. Perhaps the best way to come to grips with the problem of peering into the future in regard to this question is to review the changes that have been taking place in the media and take a realistic view of what has actually been happening to public relations in relation to those changes.

The biggest change, which we have all heard about, is the development of cable TV and the prospects for cable TV in the next 10 years. All the figures indicate that cable will grow by at least five times by the end of the decade. Cable has now reached about 10 per cent of the potential market for the service and supposedly will fill 50 or 60 per cent of the market by 1980.

Not long ago I was at a seminar devoted largely to elec—
tronic media and its prospects for the future. I was asked
what top management people are thinking about cable TV,
and the many opportunities being created by this significant
media development. I had to confess that I had had practic—
ally no conversations with presidents of companies and
very few with public relations people about this new segment
of the communications world. Those present at the seminars
couldn't understand how management could ignore the most
exciting, important, promising, dramatically changing situa—
tion in the current media picture.

I now believe that for a variety of reasons the advent
of cable TV no matter how rapidly it will develop in the
next few years, will have comparatively little effect on the
practice of public relations. I don't doubt that the prophets
are correct when they predict an amazing growth for this
new medium, and this will undoubtedly provide new outlets
of some importance to the public relations man. There will
be an added dimension to our work but not a fundamental
change. The 20 to 100 channels that may become available
through cable TV will simply provide more places for a
public relations man to present his material.

A new medium that might one day bring about a new
revolution in communications is cartridge TV. As with cable
TV, however, it's going to take quite a while before we
really see what's going to happen in that field. Some who
were premature in their expectations set up major companies
to capitalize on the cartridge TV revolution and then went
out of business because the revolution failed to take place

94

on schedule. I don't see as yet many changes in our work developing from that field.

Another dramatic change being talked about today in the media has to do with the technological developments in newspapers. This is moving so rapidly that many now foresee the day when daily newspapers will actually be generated in one's home. We in the public relations field find this as fascinating to contemplate as anybody else, but so far there is no evidence to suggest that these developments will result in any great changes in the way we do our business.

Technological changes in book publishing––such as microfilm––also promise to alter that medium radically. Book publishing can be an important factor in public relations programming, but I don't think the technological developments in this field will be any more significant to PR than the development in newspaper publishing.

Radio is another medium that has become more specialized in recent years. There are now 135 black stations, 83 Spanish language stations, 10 farm stations, over a thousand stations that carry country music exclusively, and a great many all–news stations. Ten years ago, or even five years ago, the segmentation was not nearly that well defined. Now there are at least theoretically, new opportunities for concentrated programs of communications for clients who want to reach specialized audiences. But as with cable TV, I can't think of a single instance so far in which this new pattern in radio broadcasting has been a major factor in a PR program.

Film has become one of the most creative media of our time, and there are always new directions to watch. Some

95

of the most promising innovations can be seen in art films shown as part of museum exhibitions and film workshops. But there are still too few outlets for outstanding films that have a public relations purpose. One shudders to think how many films there are in cans on the shelves of public relations departments, and I think we have a long way to go before we know how to fully take advantage of the medium of film for public relations.

When we look at magazines as specialized publications, however, the story is quite different. The changes in the magazine publishing world during the past several years has already affected the public relations business. Not long ago public relations people thought a story in *Life* magazine was about as promising an achievement as they could imagine. Many clients including corporations, governments, universities, cultural institutions were convinced that a story in *Life* magazine would solve all their problems. They would put enormous pressure on us to work towards such a story. Of course the expectations of what would happen once a *Life* story appeared were highly unrealistic. Clients' problems were not solved by such a miracle, and the disappointment was often fatal. We discovered that more often than we liked to remember, when we did get the story we lost the client. This happened so often that we used to say where there's *Life,* there's death.

Now we no longer have *Life* or *Look* or the *Saturday Evening Post.* We do have the *Reader's Digest* and *Time* and *Newsweek* as important national media to work with, but somehow even these don't hold the same glamour that *Life* once had and we don't have the same pressure on us to try to interest these magazines in articles about our clients.

In recent years there has been a tremendous upsurge in specialized magazines—something like 700 new magazines in the last 10 years. There has also been tremendous growth in newsletters and a variety of specialized publications that come into being almost overnight. Within three months after the energy crisis became a major concern (with the initiation of the oil embargo in October, 1973) six newsletters appeared dealing with energy: *Energy User's Report, Weekly Energy Report, Washington Energy Memo, Capital Energy Letter, Energy Today,* and just plain *Energy.* There had to be sufficient interest among a specialized audience for these newsletters to spring up and not overlap each other.

Changing reading patterns now make it possible for a whole series of publications to emerge in a specialized field. This is a phenomenon which first became apparent in the late 1960's and appears to be increasingly pronounced in the 1970's. And it has had a significant effect on public relations practice. If, for instance, a public relations program is developed for a company with strong energy or environmental concerns, the specialized media in those fields can be of crucial importance—not only as outlets for news about company activities, but as inputs for constructive or critical thinking about the company's public responsibilities in those areas. It is the function of thoughtful public relations people to make sure that the editor or the reporter whose writing may affect his client has access to the top management when he wants it, and that top management will be forthright and open in speaking to journalists.

In other words, the public relations function in regard to

specialized media has become more than ever to bring editor and management together so that both can do their job more effectively as a result of fruitful exchange.

When considering the importance of specialized print media in public relations programs, we must ask how much time subscribers are able to spend reading the periodicals they receive.

I recently made a note of how much time I spend reading periodicals and how many periodicals actually come across my desk and at my home on a regular basis. I found that I spend no more than an hour a day reading publications and a good deal of that is newspaper reading. And yet I regularly receive over 50 journals! These include six professional public relations publications, 14 special interest publications dealing with the arts, and 10 general magazines, and more than 20 others which come either to my home or to my office and which I desperately try to look at if not read.

What does that mean in regard to the communications effectiveness of these media? The market statistics of these publications undoubtedly show me as a reader. Yet all I can do with most of them is to scan the pages––to have some general idea of what's in them. I actually read only a very, very few articles.

Recently a friend of mine told me about an article he remembers reading in *Harper's* magazine 40 years ago that not only made a great impression on him, but probably changed the course of his life. The way I "read" *Harper's* or any other magazine today, I would think it next to impossible for me to be so profoundly affected by an article. I don't take the time to give it a chance.

98

I assume my experience is not unique, and that while it is true that people are exposed to more publications these days, they read fewer articles in depth.

In public relations terms this means that the prestige of national exposure is still important to clients, and that there are many national magazines such as *Time, Newsweek, U.S. News, Harper's, Atlantic, The Saturday Review* in which articles about clients can be significant. There are also many general women's magazines, Washington publications and several national newspapers— the *Washington Post, The New York Times,* the *Christian Science Monitor,* the *Los Angeles Times,* of which can be of almost equal importance. The prestige of major national media is still a key factor in our clients' thinking. But we must realize the message of such articles may not be communicated to their readers by the mere fact of their publication. What is important in a public relations program is that the article did appear. In that sense, the prestige of the medium is a good part of the message that gets communicated. To communicate the rest of the message and increase the probability that at least some key members of the audience read the article, a good job of mailing reprints must be done. An old adage of public relations is that half the job is getting the article in print, the other half is what you do with it once it's published. How you merchandise that article can be more important than having it published in the first place. *This rule is going to become more important than ever as specialized media proliferates.*

A recent publication entitled *Foundations and Public Information* is an outstanding example of such an effort.

Published by The Council on Foundations its purpose was to call to the attention of various thought leaders in the country what the press was reporting about the function of foundations in our society, and also to make the point that foundations were attempting to fulfill their public responsibility by issuing full reports to the press about their grants in various fields. "American Foundations," the publication stated on its cover, "have become increasingly responsive to the public's desire to understand more clearly the role of private philanthropy in today's society. More and more foundation programs are described to the press, thought leaders, and government representatives. This marked acceleration in the performance of good public information practices is indicated in some measure by the examples of editorial coverage given to foundations." The contents of the publication consisted of reprints of articles that had recently appeared in such publications as *Nation's Business, The Los Angeles Times, The Christian Science Monitor* and many other local and specialized media.

The message of the reprint was not that foundations have been getting a lot of publicity. The message was that foundations are being conscientious about getting their story to the public and in being accountable to the public. This was one important fact to bring to the attention of Congress and others concerned about the accountability of foundations. The articles in the publications themselves were not enough for this message to be communicated; only by reprinting them together and addressing them specifically to a limited audience could the story be told.

This is particularly true in regard to articles that are

100

published in specialized media. For instance, the most important article in *Foundations and Public Information* may not have been the one that appeared in the *Christian Science Monitor*, the *United Press International*, the *Los Angeles Times*, or *Nation's Business*; but rather an article in the *New York Law Journal*, a very specialized publication. This article was entitled "Private Foundations Major Factor in Aiding Criminal Justice System." Calling this to the attention of people who don't read the *Law Journal* but are interested in Foundations was an important service.

I can give a more personal example of the importance of reprints. Not long ago, I wrote an article called "Modifying Opinions in the New Human Climate" which was published in *Public Relations Quarterly*. Our firm reprinted it as one of our "R&F Papaers," and sent it to universities, heads of companies and to other people we thought would be interested in our ideas about public relations. As a result of that mailing, we received a call from the public relations director of a major company. "Would you or one associates come out and see me?" he said. "I just read your article, and I would like to assess the performance of our public relations department in terms of what you wrote in your article." One of my associates did visit the public relations director, and we had ourselves a new client—something that never would have happened if we hadn't reprinted the article.

Are specialized media becoming an important part of public relations planning? My guess is that the increasing role of such media may be one of the most significant influences on the current practice of public relations——

at least the press relations function of PR. By way of illustration, I can point to one of our clients, The Medic Alert Foundation. This is a non—profit organization that serves people with potential emergency medical problems such as penicillin allergy, diabetes, a heart condition, glaucoma. If one has an accident the bracelet he or she wears alerts a policeman or doctor to his medical problem and provides a telephone number which can be called for a complete medical file which is constantly maintained on a computer. There are now approximately 600,000 members of Medic Alert and about 50,000 or 60,000 join each year. Some of the magazines in which Medic Alert articles have appeared as a result of its PR program are *Catholic Digest, Travel Digest, Flagship News* of American Airlines, American Association of Retired Persons *Newsletter*, the American Society of Travel Agents convention newspaper, Stanley Home Products catalogue, *Holiday Inn Magazine, Volunteer Leader* (for hospital volunteers across the country), *Business Week, Yachting, The American Diabetes Association Magazine, Grit, VIP,* Playboy Club Key Members Magazine, a newsletter published by a travel club, Veteran of Foreign War's Magazine, *American Girl,* Knight's of Columbus Magazine.

A few years ago we would have been much less likely to develop a public relations program with these media in mind. Now it is becoming commonplace, and I suspect this trend is going to increase greatly as time goes by. Specialized publications will, therefore, create many new opportunities in public relations; they will also make it necessary to employ effective techniques of merchandising the results.

102

The reprint is one such technique that is already of great importance, and I am sure we will develop other techniques that will be equally effective as the multiplicity of specialized media increases.

8

THE FUTURE OF PUBLIC TELEVISION AS
A SPECIALIZED ALTERNATIVE

Jack Lyle

Much is said by different persons concerning the mission of public broadcasting to provide "alternatives" to the American public. The problem is that the concept of "alternatives" varies from person to person.

Originally the institutional entities which operated these reserved television frequencies were called "educational broadcasting," a term that is considerably more restricted than "public broadcasting." However, as early as 1963 Wilbur Schramm, Ithiel de Sola Pool and I pointed out that "educational broadcasting" was generally reaching the already educated.[1] The emphasis of prime time content by then had begun a major shift, from instructional to cultural and information programming. The metamorphosis, if indeed it was that, subsequently became official. The nomenclature used by stations to describe themselves changed from "educational" to "public" broadcasting.

A milestone of major importance was passed with the enactment of the Public Broadcasting Act of 1967. This provided for an infusion of federal money into the system and, coincidentally, established the Corporation for Public

104

Broadcasting which subsequently organized national inter-connections to serve the locally licensed and controlled public stations. The interconnection for TV was the Public Broadcasting Service, PBS, for radio it was National Public Radio, NPR.

The enactment of the Public Broadcasting Act was a milestone, not the millenium. As is so frequently the case in this imperfect world, federal financial support was not obtained without accompanying problems. This is not the place to discuss those problems. The present point is that the Act did introduce new participants in the discussion of "alternative" programming. Members of the Congress and the Administration now had reason to take part in the discussion: federal funds were involved. The fact that funds from the general federal treasury were involved implied to minority and action groups that public stations should have particular responsibilities to the public—which they usually translated to mean their own segment of the public. The interest of the Congress and the Administration made media critics and commentators more alert and sensitive to the possibilities of political pressures in the selection of alternatives. Educational broadcasting now had become public broadcasting in the sense that it was a matter of public discussion—whether it had an audience or not.

The discussion on the subject, particularly over the past two years, has frequently seemed to generate more heat than understanding and agreement. For those working in or truly concerned with public broadcasting the discus-sions have been neither easy nor comforting, yet they have not been without benefits. Who knows, they may yet lead to some agreement on the question of "alternative" service and programming. But there is also the danger that the smoke thrown up by these discussions and press comment will divert public scrutiny away from the far greater question of the appropriate role of commercial broadcasting in this country. The concept of public television as an "alternative" service is a perfectly valid one. However, I would argue that it should not be used to relieve the major broadcasting system, the commercial system, from the responsibility also to provide alternatives.

I risk belaboring this point because of the constraints under which the public broadcasting system must operate and the implications of those constraints for the development of "alternatives." Let me review the major constraints.

First and of overriding importance is the fact that, despite its unique nature, public broadcasting does operate within the context of a competitive broadcasting market. The vast majority of the population of the United States lives in markets where they have simultaneous availability of the three major commercial television networks, one or more "independent" commercial stations, a public television station, plus a considerable number of AM and FM radio signals, which may include a public station. Viability for a commercial station is based on numbers. Programming which can attract a large audience has commercial viability. Programs which can attract a large audience have commercial value.

The implication of this truism for public broadcasters is important and perhaps not very pleasant. It is the prob—

bability that public broadcasting will be forced to be content with minority audiences, minority in the sense of smaller numbers as compared to those of the commercial system.

A lesson which has been learned by FM stations and which is being learned by independent television station operators is that large minorities can be commercially attractive to selective advertisers. As the number of television channels has increased in urban markets, a competition has developed for not just the majority audiences, but also for large minority audiences. Pushed to its logical extreme, a thesis that public broadcasting is charged with providing an alternative to commercial broadcasting means that the public broadcasters are left with only the audiences that as yet have not proven a viable base for commercial exploitation.

Public broadcasters have not—and I hope will not—settle for that extreme position. Another, more positive, line of thought is that public broadcasting has the responsibility, the opportunity to be the experimental stage on which new and varied programming ideas can be tested and demonstrated. In this framework, success is measured by the extent to which the idea or format is copied by the commercial broadcasters. This thesis has the rather sad conclusion that the fruit of success is the loss or at least a sharing of the audience to the commercial broadcasters. We have already seen examples of this with some of the dramatic presentations. The "Six Wives of Henry VIII" was first shown on CBS and then public television, as was also the more recent case with the Joseph Papp production of "Much Ado About Nothing." "Elizabeth R", on the other hand, first appeared in this country on PBS and was then shown on some commercial stations.

Between these positions is the possibility of an alternative programming which provides a special function either for the general audience or for specially defined groups within the population. The most outstanding successes in this area probably are the children's programs. Whether or not one approves of the pedagogical objectives of "Sesame Street", it must be admitted that the evidence shows the program has been able to attract viewers of a specified age within the competitive market and to achieve specific results among those viewers.

Another success has been "Zoom", the program by and for pre-teen youngsters. Inspection of the demographic analysis in the Nielson reports for individual markets shows that although the overall rating of this show is small by commercial standards, among pre-teens it generally has the second largest audience in its prime time slot. The program which outpoints it pulls a large general, family audience while "Zoom's" audience is primarily drawn from the elementary school age group. This spotlights another problem which alternative programming for specific groups must face: competition for control of the set. Although multiple set households are increasing, most evening viewing continues to be family viewing. In such situations alternative programs for specific audience segments are at a disadvantage compared to a program of more general appeal.

A point to be kept in mind is that such terms as "mass", "minority" and "small" are all relative. For instance, the standard audience "ratings" are actually in terms of the per cent of the nation's households which tune in a program. Highly successful commercial programs have ratings in the high 20's and beyond. A program that does not achieve a rating of at least 12 is a sure candidate for cancellation.

By contrast the highest rating for any national public television program last season was between 6 and 7. That sounds very small by commercial standards, but projected against a population of over 60 million households, it means that over three million families were watching. In a nation the size of ours, a "minority" or "small" audience can actually be a "mass" audience.

As an aside it should also be noted that public television programs suffer a discounting when the ratings are used as a standard of success. Many public TV stations are handicapped by UHF channel allocations, many––including VHF stations––are handicapped by inadequate transmitter equipment. Because of limitations of transmission techno-ogy it is estimated that perhaps 25 per cent of the nation's homes actually do not have the option of watching simply because they can't get a decent signal for the nearest public station.

The fact remains, however, that public television audiences are "relatively" small. By Nielson estimate, the majority of the prime time national programs have audiences of less than one million homes. At the local level the audiences of some programs––both national and locally produced––slip to figures which are truly disturb-ingly small. Whatever the legitimacy of the "alternative" they are providing, beyond some point one must raise the

109

question of the appropriateness of open broadcast signals as a distribution means. This critical point is more quickly reached in television than radio, due to the higher operating costs and the relatively fewer frequency availabilities. This question will become more and more pressing for television in the future as cable and some form of video cassette or recording availability spread through the population.

It should be emphasized that the ratings of individual programs should not be used as indicators of the total audience of public broadcasting. There is considerable evidence to support the thesis that the audiences of public broadcasting programs tend to be discrete audiences, audiences which turn to the channel for a specific program and perhaps only that program during the entire week. For a commercial station or network broadcasters this situation would be intolerable, a sure sign of financial doom. But for an "alternative service" it need not be fatal. As stated earlier, an operational assumption is that the public broadcasting audience will be "relatively" small, although we certainly wish they were not as small as they are. Perhaps a more critical factor from the standpoint of the nature of public broadcasting's bases of support, is not the size of individual programs but the cumulative audience over time, say a week. If public television is providing an alternative for large proportions of the nation's homes even once or a few times a week, an argument can be made that it is achieving success.

As a matter of fact, the few studies which have been done to date strongly suggest that station memberships and individual contributions do reflect a type of appreciation of value received. The special presentation of the film of Nureyev's production of the ballet "Sleeping Beauty" brought in thousands of new "members." More dramatic was the influx of gifts and new memberships generated by the prime time presentation of the Watergate Hearings. The point, of course, is that the more specialized interest groups which can find attractive alternatives on public broadcasting, the greater potential for development of direct viewer support.

Unfortunately, alternatives for certain groups, specific—ally the underprivileged ethnic minorities, are unlikely to generate such financial response for the simple reason that the audience served is unlikely to have the resources to provide such response. But their numbers can help swell the cumulative audience as an argument for the justification of public, foundation, or corporate support.

Compilation of cumulative audience estimates for the season now nearing an end is still in process. Last season the figures, based on Nielson national ratings, indicated that about one fourth of the nation's families watched at least one public television program during the week. Something under a third of that audience was composed of children viewing the daytime programs, many——if not most——of whom view on a daily basis. Prime time national programming was reaching somewhere around 18% of the homes and most of these viewed only one program a week. Over a two—month period the prime time cumulative audience increased to 36% of the homes. The preliminary unofficial figures for this year is 40%, a 13% growth.

111

Analysis of demographic data on the audience, both from Nielsen figures and from special studies, indicates that there is more socio—economic spread in public television's audience than had generally been supposed. However, the greatest success public television has had in attracting lower income and minority homes has been achieved through the children's programs, not programs for the adult audience. Thus, if public broadcasting is to throw off the stigma of elitism, it must increase not just the size of audience of individual programs, but the cumulative reach. At present, the "strongest" stations are reaching a weekly total of about 50% ——so even in those markets there is room for growth.

Critics of public broadcasting do not always acknowledge the complexity of this problem of audience vis a vis the competitive program environment. Programming decisions on public affairs and minority presentations are generally discussed by these critics solely on political terms. Those making the decisions undoubtedly wish matters were that simple, but they are not.

Audience data over the years has consistently shown that the prime time programs which attract the largest audience are the cultural programs of drama, music and dance. Not only do cultural programs as a group attract almost twice as many viewers as do public affairs programs as a group, but the individual programs have larger audiences. In the 1972—73 season William Buckley's "Firing Line" was the only public affairs program which consistently was among the top five PBS programs in Nielsen terms. Further, stations have documented that the cultural programs

112

are the top producers of viewer and membership support. The great exception to this, of course, was the presentation of the Watergate Hearings. Similarly, it should be noted that on a local level in several markets investigative reporting–type local news programs have scored well both in terms of audience size and financial support. But these programs also tend to be expensive and it must be confessed they are having difficulty surviving as initial foundation support has been phased out.

Minority programming is an extremely complex question. Not only have the minority programs presented thus far on public television generally drawn very small ratings, special studies have indicated that they have attracted only a minority of the minorities involved. A survey of urban blacks, for instance, reported that 15% said they watched "Black Journal" regularly and less than half said they had ever viewed the program. The more entertainment–oriented program, "Soul", attracted larger numbers.[2]

What is a minority program? This is a critical question with which programmers are only now seeking to come to grips. There is ample data to document that minorities are not monolithic groups. Like all groups, their members span a broad range of attitudes and program preferences; regional differences and jealousies are evident. That there is a compelling necessity for minority programming is not ques–tioned, but neither is the necessity to make such program–ming as beneficial as possible to as many as possible.

All the foregoing discussion comes to focus in the area of audience research. It is perhaps ironic that public broad–casting, with its much more limited resources, should actually be faced with problems in audience measurement which far exceed those of the commercial stations.

We are evolving a research strategy, the emerging shape of which I will outline here. Our goal is a research loop consisting of four basic elements or phases: (1) ascertainment, (2) developmental, (3) evaluative and (4) synthesis.

Although the Federal Communications Commission is only now debating making ascertainment of community needs a requirement for non—commercial broadcasters, many public stations have already been attempting to do that. The Corporation (but not all the other entities within the public broadcasting family) has replied to the FCC that it feels public broadcasters do have a particular responsibility to engage in ascertainment, although it also feels that the limited resources available to most of these stations must be taken into account in stipulating any specific requirements.

From the FCC's standpoint, ascertainment is intended to stimulate a broader use of broadcasting resources for ameliorating problems affecting the community or segments of the community. In effect, this is a public service approach. But ascertainment can also be looked at as a means of identifying needs and interests which might be used as a basis for attracting specialized audiences to the alternative programming on public broadcasting. This is the type of activity which Lloyd Morrisett has referred to in his essay, "RX for Public Broadcasting."[4] It becomes an operational problem of matching potential alternatives in programming with such interests.

But the problem does not stop there. Public broadcast—

114

ing's "alternatives" must still compete with a variety of commercial programs which themselves may have high appeal to members of the special interest group being sought. Thus it is not enough to identify a potential interest group, but other information also must be obtained in order to effectively promote and schedule the program if it is to have a chance of success: i.e., to reach a respectable percentage of those for whom it is intended.

Developmental research activities should assist those responsible for the design and production of the program content of public broadcasting, providing them objective checks on appropriateness of decisions concerning creative activities. In the broadcast media, those responsible for programming do not have the benefit of a natural immediate feedback loop from the intended audience. Audience ratings may ultimately provide a quantitative measure of success or failure, but unfortunately the nature of the medium requires considerable "lead time" between production and actual broadcast. Developmental research is an attempt to bridge that time gap.

Program production is a creative process and such processes inevitably rely heavily on intuition, aesthetic principles, expertise. But those in themselves may not be sufficient, particularly for those engaged in developing experimental program approaches for specialized audiences. The nature of the broadcast media means a spatial—and usually a temporal—gulf between creator and audience. Production is expensive and resources always limited. Those in charge of programming need objective means by which to validate the results of the creative processes.

The fact that many public broadcasting programs seek to do more than entertain creates a double burden. If it is assumed that programs and series do have stipulated goals for stipulated audiences, there should be objective testing at the time of production to guarantee that "the message" is made explicit and to attempt to gauge competitive viability.

Today the term "formative" research generally is applied to this activity when connected with development of program format and content. Considerable impetus for this type of research has been provided by the success of the Children's Television Workshop's "Sesame Street." As public broadcasters increasingly focus on "alternative programs" of a specific nature for specific audiences, the research lesson of "Sesame Street" is gaining increasing acceptance. It must be admitted that as one moves into the field of cultural and public affairs programming, two fields of particular importance for public broadcasting, it becomes harder to pinpoint specific objectives. That difficulty, however, must not be used as an excuse to bypass formative research in these areas.

The ultimate success of any message is whether or not it reaches its intended audience and achieves the intended impact upon that audience. This is the function of evaluative research. A simple "counting of the house" in terms of the number in the audience no longer suffices even in commercial broadcasting, where advertisers have become increasingly sensitive to the demographic composition of audiences. For public broadcasters "counting the house" is an even less satisfactory evaluative measure. The very real constraints imposed upon public broadcasting means,

116

as we have noted repeatedly, that the audience of its programs generally will be small relative to those of the commercial stations.

If public broadcasting's goal is alternative programming for specific groups, the appropriate measure is not the percent of the total population which uses the program, but the percent of the "target" group. The question of audience composition thus is of overriding importance for public broadcasting.

This is not to say that public broadcasting is not concerned with numbers. Numbers must be of concern, particularly to CPB. Since the funds the Corporation administers are provided primarily from the public purse, it must be concerned with providing the most effective service possible for as many people as possible. This does not mean attempting to draw the largest possible proportion of the total population to any given program, but rather that over time specific services are provided to groups which in combination will represent a large proportion of the public. As I said earlier, public broadcasters can tolerate relatively small audiences for individual programs *if* the cumulative audience is large. Ideally, our weekly cume should be 100%.

Further, one must always be alert to serendipitous effects which a program may achieve. Such effects, which may be found in looking at general as opposed to specific audience data, provide suggestions for fruitful avenues of program expansion or development of new programs.

Another dimension of evaluative research is "summative" research which seeks to determine if the program is achieving its intended effect among those who do view.

This does become more difficult as one moves from programs of highly specific content to those tied to more general goals or content. Again, while the primary concern is with the effect upon the specified audience, one should be alert to possible effects on other groups in the population.

Finally there is synthesis, the putting together of all the pieces. Research with direct or indirect relevance to the problems of public broadcasting are undertaken on local initiative as well as under the guidance and support of CPB. Pertinent studies are also undertaken within the academic community. General studies of the population by commercial research groups and, indeed, by the commercial broadcasting industry frequently contain information relevant to the problems of public broadcasting.

CPB is seeking to gather together as many of these bits and pieces as possible, to provide wider dissemination of findings and implications, to provide occasional synthesis of findings for the general benefit of the entire public broadcasting industry and, finally, to promote the coordination of individual efforts to create a bank of compatible data which will be available to all interested researchers through a public broadcasting data archive.

In a 1973 talk I concluded with a dismal observation that the prevailing system of media research in this country focused on studying the audience for the benefit of the communication industry, not for improving the service provided to the public.

Within public broadcasting we are attempting to develop research that is audience—oriented. If public broadcasting

118

is to survive, it must seek to serve rather than exploit the public. Perhaps that is the most meaningful significance to the concept of public broadcasting as an alternative service.

---

[1] Wilbur Schramm, Ithiel de Sola Pool, and Jack Lyle, *The People Look at Educational Television* (Stanford: Stanford University Press, 1963).

[2] Jack Lyle, *Public Television and the Urban Black Audience* (Washington: Corporation for Public Broadcasting, 1973).

[3] Nicholas Valenzuela, *Public Television and the Mexican-American Audience in the Southwest*, (Washington: Corporation for Public Broadcasting, 1974).

[4] See the 1972–73 Annual Report of the John and Mary R. Markle Foundation.

PART III. THE NEW MEDIA

For many years now, futurists have been telling us that the day of the wired nation is at hand, and that such technology will make more specialization feasible not only in television but also in newspapers. Cable television and computer connections, they say, soon will connect homes not only with television stations but also with banks, supermarkets, health services, and most governmental agencies. The cable also will allow people to interact via television and will make possible printing of facsimile newspapers in the home.

The promise of the technology, however, so far has surpassed its results——not because of technological limitations but because of the shortcomings of the institutions which control and regulate the technology.

In 1970, a report of the cable television commission set up by the Alfred P. Sloan Foundation traced the development of cable television through the stages of providing television where none was available, to providing more channels to areas where television existed, to providing a substitute medium for broadcast television where reception was poor. In the future, the report concluded, cable will

120

complement rather than substitute for over–the air–television. The new "television of abundance" will, like the printing press, provide more channels for more specialized content and will free the medium from the economic constraints of advertisers, readers, or any other *single* source of revenue.[1]

Jones, in first chapter of Part III, explores the future of interactive cable television. He lists a series of social, economic, and political consequences of people interacting with government, stores and libraries via the picture tube. Most importantly, he points out, interactive television will affect the way people spend their time. Generally, Jones predicts, they will spend less time with conventional television, less time sleeping and less time in social activities.

The cable and computers attached to it may also make a new style of life possible––that of "telecommuting." Nilles describes this possibility in the second chapter of Part III. Through the use of telecommunications, people may some day be able to work in or near their homes and communicate with fellow workers or a central office through the computer and over the cable. Nilles describes research conducted at the University of Southern California which thus far shows that telecommuting is already economically and technologically feasible.

Any new medium will have a great impact upon existing media, and one of the most important of these influences is economic. McCombs, in Chapter 11, discusses how a Principle of Relative Constancy explains the amount of money people spend on media and how it can predict what

121

cable and casette TV will do to the economic support of existing media. The principle shows that the amount of money spent on media has been a constant proportion of Gross National Product over time. Therefore, money spent on new media must come either from money spent on other media or from increased incomes. McCombs says some money for new media could come from new sources not utilized by existing media, such as banks or businesses which would use the cable as a common carrier, as they now use the telephone, but he adds that most of the money probably would come from money now spent on newspapers and television.

One important constraint on cable television has come from the regulatory policy of the Federal Communications Commission. Previous chapters in this section have shown that cable technology will compete with the technology of the broadcast television industry and of the print media. Recent history of FCC regulation, however, in general has restricted the development of cable TV and has afforded protection to existing broadcasters serving the top television markets.[2] Owen for example, has argued that because of the economics of the television industry cable television should be made a common carrier, like a telephone line available to anyone who pays to use it, if cable technology is to be used to its full potential.[3]

In a major report on cable television, Adler has presented a case for the "humanistic claim on the cable." Without new means of economic support, he pointed out, the cable could simply be a new technology which will make a "vast wasteland even vaster." He, too, argued that economics

122

has determined the content of present—day television. Good drama appeared on television early in its development, he says, because then only the affluent could afford a television set and because good drama appealed to this wealthy and better educated audience. Cable operators alone, he concluded, will not be able to support diversified programming on the cable so support will have to come from new sources such as pay cable or gifts and grants.[4]

Chapters 12 and 13 put these new media into perspective. Katzman turns our attention to the overall impact of new communication technology on society. He concludes that new information technology, like many new technological innovations, will probably improve the position of the "information rich" relative to the position of the "information poor." The poor may gain in an absolute sense but not at as fast a rate as will the rich.[5]

Price, in Chapter 14, also cautions that many of the promises of the "dream machine" of cable television will not come to fruition. According to Price, cable advocates predict that the cable will "eliminate scarcity" and the "monopoly status of the programmer" and that its many channels will "allow competing views to find an audience." But cable still has not approached these promises, he concludes, largely because of the inadequacies of such institutions as schools and health services which might expand their services through the cable.[6]

---

1. The Sloan Commission on Cable Television, *On the Cable: The Television of Abundance* (New York: McGraw—Hill, 1971).

2. Ralph Lee Smith, "CATV: FCC Rules and the Public

Interest,'' in George Gerbner, et al., *Commucication Technology and Social Policy* (New York: John Wiley & Sons, 1973), pp. 124–131.

3. Bruce M. Owen, ''Public Policy and Emerging Technology in the Media,'' *Public Policy* 18 (1970): pp. 539–552.

4. Richard Adler, ''The Humanistic Claim on the Cable,'' in Richard Adler and Walter S. Baer, *The Electronic Box Office* (New York: Praeger Publishers, 1974) : pp. 1–17.

5. This general conclusion must be tempered, however, by a recent finding of Donohue, Tichenor, and Olien. In a study of a small Minnesota community, they found a ''knowledge gap on a national news item, but no such gap on an information item locally relevant to that community.'' In other words, a knowledge gap does not exist for information of direct importance to them. G. A. Donohue, P. J. Tichenor, and C. W. Olien, ''Mass Media and the Knowledge Gap: A Hypothesis Reconsidered,'' *Communication Research* 2 (1975): 3–23.

6. Parker has concluded, in a similar fashion, that research is needed not on new technology itself but on the institutions which will control and utilize that technology. Edwin B. Parker, ''Implications of New Information Technology,'' *Public Opinion Quarterly* 37 (1973–74): 590–600.

9

CABLE TV AS AN INTERACTIVE MEDIUM
OF THE FUTURE

Martin V. Jones

New engineering developments in television, computers, and related technologies will soon make possible a revo— lutionizing of the nation's electronic communications systems. At that time, homes, businesses, educational institutions, government agencies and community organ— izations can be linked by pictures and sound in the same way that telephone today links them by voice. These electronic innovations will not only make it possible for people in widely separated locations to simultaneously

---

The matters discussed in this paper are reported in more detail in a MITRE Corporation paper written by the author, entitled ''How Interactive Television Will Affect the Way We Live: An Initial Assessment'' M73—20 (February 1973). An abstract of this longer report containing more statistical detail than the present paper appeared in the October 1973 issue of the *Futurist* magazine entitled ''How Cable Television May Change Our Lives.''

view a physical object about which they are conversing, they will also enable users to retrieve, almost instantaneously, information stored in libraries, central data banks and remote files.

These electronic innovations, then, which for convenience I have termed interactive television (TV), will bring huge amounts of information into a person's home or office and give that person the ability to respond, immediately, with his own ideas. These innovations in two—way communications will profoundly affect the way that men live.

To date, the relatively limited funds available for researching interactive TV have gone to improving the engineering details of the technology, itself, and to planning for future experimental applications of the interactive medium in pilot—test communities. For the most part, little systematic study has been made of the likely social impacts of interactive television.

Many authorities have predicted, however, that the widespread introduction of interactive cable TV into the nation's major population centers will have tremendous social impacts. For instance, Arthur L. Singer, Jr., Vice President of the Sloan Commission, has stated that the cable wiring of major cities . . .

> will carry with it social, political, and
> economic implications of unparalleled
> significance, dwarfing the changes that
> were brought about by such earlier
> developments as the development of
> television itself or by the creation of the
> present highway network.[1]

126

What might some of these implications be? We can be certain, for starters, that literally hundreds of uses would be found for this new technology. Among the many new capabilities that citizens and organizations would have are the following:

1. An ability to access filed documents from libraries, offices and other sources instantly.
2. An ability to conduct and participate in nationwide electronic voting surveys and political referendums.
3. An ability to compile a "dedicated" newspaper or magazine——that is, one containing information specifically tailored to one's own personal interests or needs.
4. An ability to send and receive mail electronically.
5. An ability to obtain a remote medical diagnosis.

The applications of interactive TV could be expected to lead, eventually, to widespread changes in many areas of life. Let us for a moment assume that by 1980 or 1990 interactive television does, in fact, become installed in 50 percent of the residences, industries and government offices in the nation's major, non—rural areas . . . . Here are just a few of the first—level impacts that such a system might have:

1. Citizens will be better informed.
2. Public officials will be more responsive to the electorate.
3. Government services will be disseminated more equitably.

4. Specialized medical, legal and other professional skills will be available to larger numbers of people
5. Communication within an organization and between organizations will be faster.
6. The nation's workforce will be better trained.
7. Shopping will be more convenient for consumers.

The cumulative, ultimate effects of these initial impacts will be:

1. The total volume of societal communications will increase: within business and government, within communities, among people at all levels.
2. Political candidates will have an easier access to voters.
3. There will be a trend toward "participatory" as opposed to "representative" government.
4. The siting for education will be decentralized.
5. It will be easier for minority interest groups to reach their members, each other, and the rest of society.
6. There will be greater problems in controlling defamation, fraud and obscenity.
7. The role of the postal service in servicing the nation's transactions and correspondence needs will be lessened.
8. Additional anti—monopoly problems may arise from cross—media ownership.
9. Copyright litigation may increase and the pressure to undertake a major overhaul of the nation's copyright laws may increase.

128

10. There may be a shift in local advertising from newspapers to TV.
11. The possibilities for electronic theft and for invasion of privacy will increase greatly.

At this time, of course, no one can really say how large the market for interactive television is likely to become, or, for that matter, how soon it will begin to reach its potential. Several years ago, however, in a market study for the Institute of the Future, economist Paul Baran predicted that by 1989 there will be a $20 billion annual market for two—way home information services.[2] This anticipated market would be spread over 30 highly varied categories, the largest category (video library services) representing about 15 percent of the total.

Several things about Baran's projections should be noted. First, the magnitude of this potential economic impact can be gauged by the fact that the $20 billion sum approximately equals what consumers currently spend for all electricity and telephone services combined.

As large as this projected sum is, it still omits certain important areas of consumer impact. For instance, Baran did not include any health applications. Although most remote medical—diagnosis applications of interactive TV would not take place in the home, millions of citizens are likely to participate in such applications.

Also, the dollar impact may be a poor indicator of the real social impact in the case of some applications. For instance, although the dollar value of interactive TV services involved in instant citizen voting and referendums may never be large, the political ramifications of such an application could be profound.

It is evident that if interactive television is to be widely applied, many engineering, economic, legal and political problems will have to be surmounted. Of all the considerations that will impact on the success of interactive TV, however, few are at once as important, as intriguing and as little understood as its effect on the way people live.

Paul Baran examined interactive TV in terms of dollars. My approach has been to analyze the growth and possibilities of interactive TV in terms of *time*——your time and mine. My analysis addresses this question: how will citizens find the time to use interactive television extensively?

The relevance of a time—budget analysis is to be found in consumer motivations and life styles. Frequently, consumers, especially those in middle and upper income brackets, will willingly spend more money *and* at the same time accept a lower quality product in order to save time. One example is the tremendous popularity of TV dinners and other precooked foods.

This characteristic of modern living, that people lead brim—filled, busy lives, is also evidenced by the fact that they frequently buy more books, newspapers and magazines than they find time to read. They would like to engage in five or six hobbies or active sports but have time for only two or three. Most parents would like to spend more time with their children than they do. Many people say that they would devote more time to community, church, or professional organizations if there were more hours in the day.

What all this says is this: There are only 24 hours in a day, and, for most people, these hours are occupied doing something. This means that any new way of spending time, if it is to consume a large block of the citizen's time, must displace something else.

To the extent that this is true, it will be in those instances in which interactive television can save the consumer's time that interactive television will have its greatest advantage over competitive technologies and services. On the other hand, the present lack of idle time in most people's daily schedules may constitute one of the biggest initial obstacles to people spending a lot of time with interactive television.

To estimate the eventual impacts of *widespread* interactive TV on people's time—budgets, we should, ideally, have substantial data from many carefully planned and executed *demonstration* projects. Several such projects are now either in the planning or initial execution stage, but none has progressed far enough to provide enough usable data for a broad analysis of consumer response.

Lacking this experimental data base, the next best thing would be to employ what professional forecasters call the analogy method of forecasting, one of the oldest and most widely used of all forecasting techniques. Simply stated, the analogy method uses some similar condition or event on which an information base has been accumulated as a benchmark to project the nature of some future event.

There have been many market research applications of this method. For instance, tape recorder manufacturers used statistical data describing the size and composition of the phonograph market as a basis for forecasting the market characteristics of the tape recorder. Manufacturers of hair sprays used the market statistics on other cosmetics as a basis for estimating who would buy hair sprays, and how much. The historical data on vitamin—pill usage has often been used as a benchmark in forecasting likely consumer response to other new food supplements.

The older product or technology whose historical record is used as an estimating base should be as similar as possible to the new product or technology in use character— istics. Second, there should be an ample statistical base covering the older technology.

In applying the analogy method of forecasting, I first assumed that if interactive television were to be applied widely, it would consume approximately 1—1/2 hours daily of the average citizen's time. This is the amount of time that the *average* citizen now spends with conventional, one—way television. Many people spend much more; many spend much less.

Second, as my statistical base, I used time—budget data reported by John P. Robinson in the U.S. Surgeon General's report *Television and Social Behavior*. Robinson's study furnishes breakdowns of the difference in the time budgets of those who own TV's and those who do not.

Third, I assumed that, for the most part, the time— budget trends generated by one—way television will continue when two—way, or interactive, television takes hold.

A statistical summary of my analysis appears in Figure 1. Here is how I interpret these data.

People will get the time to use interactive TV primarily by reducing the time they presently devote to one—way television, sleep, and social activity away from home.

132

Modest reductions in time spent in reading books, leisure travel, animal care and gardening, laundry, personal care, conversation, and miscellaneous leisure will also provide some of the time needed for using interactive TV.

Relatively little time for using interactive TV will come from reductions in the time devoted to active sports, other media (newspapers, magazines, and theater movies), religious activity, community and professional organizations and formal study. This conclusion is based on the fact that citizens en masse already spend relatively little time on these activities, so that there is not much room for further reductions, and on the fact that one—way TV has not made much inroad into the time that consumers spend on most of these activities.

In the long run, the time for using interactive TV could conceivably be made available as the workweek shortens and people spend less time in gainful employment. However, the limited data available does not indicate that the time for watching one—way TV has come from this source. Nor does it appear likely that a reduction in the workweek will be a major source of time for using interactive TV because:

1. A shortening in the average work hours is a rather slow process. Between 1900 and 1950 the U.S. chopped five hours off the work—week and, as productivity increases, it is expected that another five hours will be taken from the workweek by the year 2000. However, the amount of reduction in the workweek between 1973 and 1980 is not likely to average more than one hour.

A Projected Citizen Average Daily Time Budget
Assuming That 90 Minutes Per Day
Are Allotted To Interactive TV
(Estimates expressed in minutes per day)

Activities	Present Allotments		Projected Allotments	
	Those Who Do Not Own A TV	Those Who Own TVs	Interactive TV Users	Change
1. Interactive TV	0	0	90.0	+90
2. One-Way TV	11.3	87.6	72.8	−14.8
3. Main Job	253.2	254.2	254.2	0
4. Second Job	4.1	3.7	3.3	−0.4
5. At Work (Other)	10.8	10.6	10.4	−0.2
6. Travel to Work	28.4	28.1	27.8	−0.3
7. Cooking	56.7	55.0	53.3	−1.7
8. Home Chores	58.1	57.9	57.7	−0.2
9. Laundry	32.9	27.9	22.9	−5.0
10. Marketing	18.1	18.1	18.1	0
11. Animals, Garden	17.6	11.5	5.8	−5.7
12. Shopping	6.4	7.7	7.7	0
13. Other Household	20.8	19.1	17.4	−1.7
14. Child Care	16.8	17.9	17.9	0
15. Other Child	10.1	11.5	11.5	0
16. Personal Care	59.5	55.0	50.5	−4.5

17.	Eating	84.6	84.7	84.7	0
18.	Sleep	491.8	479.3	466.8	-12.5
19.	Personal Travel	19.0	18.4	17.8	-0.6
20.	Leisure Travel	20.5	16.4	12.3	-4.1
21.	Study	18.1	15.7	13.3	-2.4
22.	Religion	6.2	3.5	1.8	-1.7
23.	Organizations	3.6	5.3	5.3	0
24.	Radio	13.2	5.2	2.6	-2.6
25.	Read Newspapers	15.3	15.2	15.1	-0.1
26.	Read Magazines	5.4	3.9	2.4	-1.5
27.	Read Books	14.1	8.3	4.2	-4.1
28.	Movies	6.5	3.1	1.6	-1.5
29.	Social (Home)	11.7	14.6	14.6	0
30.	Social (Away)	33.9	22.4	11.2	-11.2
31.	Conversation	19.5	14.5	9.5	-5.0
32.	Active Sports	2.6	2.4	2.2	-0.2
33.	Outdoors	17.5	15.8	14.1	-1.7
34.	Entertainment	3.9	3.9	3.9	0
35.	Cultural Events	1.1	1.0	0.9	-0.1
36.	Resting	24.8	23.8	22.8	-1.0
37.	Other Leisure	21.9	16.7	11.5	-5.2
	TOTAL	1,440	1,440	1,440	0

First published by the author in a MITRE Corporation report (M73–20) entitled "How Interactive Television Will Affect the Way We Live: An Initial Assessment", February 1973.

135

2. Many activities, such as other media, active sports, community affairs, travel and vacations, gardening, etc., will compete with interactive TV for that extra hour of the worker's free time.

To summarize, new electronic communications systems will substantially impact on the nation's life style in the next two decades. Because these trends are only now beginning to emerge, we can only speculate as to what these specific impacts will be and when they will occur. In this paper, I have engaged in such speculation, using a limited sample of available data covering the impacts caused by conventional television as the primary basis for these projections.

---

1. Cited in *Wiring the World,* a U.S. News and World Report Book, (editor Joseph Newman), 1971.

2. Paul Baran, *Potential Market for Two—Way Information Services to the Home, 1970—90,* Institute for the Future (R—26), December 1971, p. 121.

10

TELECOMMUTING: COMMUNICATIONS AS A
SUBSTITUTE FOR COMMUTING

Jack M. Nilles

The problem of commuting is a familiar one to all of us. In most large cities in the United States, there is a twice—daily surge of traffic to and from central business districts or other major work centers. Ninety—seven percent of this urban passenger traffic uses the private automobile. Furthermore, more than forty percent of all urban trips are made by commuters. These two massive traffic surges provide the primary bases for the design of major urban highways and mass transit systems.

Our University of Southern California research team is asking if there are ways to mitigate both the daily traffic surges and the major economic impacts of new commuter oriented transportation systems through the substitution of telecommunications and computer technologies——telecommuting——for some of these trips? Is it possible to develop effective telecommunications alternatives to urban commuter travel which will have a net societal benefit?

TELECOMMUTING

Our research emphasis has been placed on three primary aspects of telecommuting. First, we have taken the attitude that, if there is to be any extensive substitution of transportation by telecommunications, there must be economic incentives on the part of individual businesses to engage in the substitution. Since technological considerations play an important part in the economics, we are attempting to identify key technological events, if any, which may be required before certain phases of the telecommuting process can be made economical. Finally, we are concerned with the effectiveness of the telecommuting process as it relates to the ability of workers to perform in this new mode and their motivation to do so. The net result of all these three considerations is being used to formulate questions of public policy at the federal, state, regional, and local levels.

INFORMATION INDUSTRIES

Those workers who could be involved in the substitution of telecommunications for transportation are primarily members of information industries. Present members of the information industry are firms such as insurance companies and others in the financial sector, educational institutions, the media, government agencies, and those engaged in administrative activities in general. Many of the people in these industries currently travel to and from central locations every business day, sit there together with their fellow workers, doing work which primarily involves interactions with some form of communications or storage system such as a computer, the mail, or some physical storage system. Many of these jobs do not require frequent face—to—face interaction with other people or the performance of physical services requiring a common central location such as for the production of goods. Since more than sixty percent of the present U.S. labor force comprises white collar and clerical workers, the great majority of whom are in information industries or information segments of other industries, it is easy to presume that telecommuting could have a significant impact on the economy and on urban life in general.

EXEMPLAR CASE STUDY

To give some focus to our research, a preliminary investigation was made of the banking and insurance industries. Arrangements were then made to perform a detailed analysis of a major national insurance company, using the regional home office administrative operations in Los Angeles as a subject. At present, slightly more than twenty—five hundred employees commute every day to a single building located in central Los Angeles. Of this total number, sixty—eight percent are clerical level workers, twenty—seven percent are in middle management, and five percent are in the top management levels. The average work round trip distance for these employees is twenty—two miles. This figure compares with a national average round trip to work distance of nineteen miles. Consequently, even though Los Angeles is generally considered as an

139

extreme example of a dispersed city, the commuting distances are only fifteen percent higher in this case than the national average.

Because of the large fraction of employees at the clerical and middle management levels, emphasis was placed on analyzing their daily communication requirements in order to develop descriptions of the potential modes of telecommuting. These requirements were then used as a basis for development for telecommuting network models, analyses of technological requirements, evaluation of capabilities, and assessment of alternative costs.

EVOLUTIONARY STEPS

The possibilities of evolution of organizational structures are interesting to review as they relate to applications of telecommunications technology and their effects on public policy. We identify four major phases of organizational evolution in this respect. The first phase, centralization, is typical of most business entities today. That is, most businesses, or at least administrative operations of those businesses, consist of a monolithic group of workers at a single central site. These workers are organizationally divided into various functional groups in terms of the primary information product associated with each function. Although many major national organizations have such offices in several parts of the country, each office can be considered as a centralized organization.

The next phase of the process is that of fragmentation, at this point, coherent subunits of the central
140

organization "break off" and relocate elsewhere. The interorganizational communications boundaries are stretched and replaced by telecommunications or mail systems, while the intraorganizational communications remain intact. Two variations of fragmentation are common. Segmenting, in which functional subunits such as data processing, accounting, marketing analysis, etc. separate from the central core, is appearing with increasing frequency and in fact has occurred for one subunit of the insurance company under study. Branching is a common form of fragmentation in the financial industry and includes those cases where the fragmented units are identical in function, if not in size and detailed organization, to the parent body.

The third phase of the process, called dispersion, involves the establishment of a series of scattered business locations of the firm in which the organizational subunits as well as the employees are dispersed. That is, an employee reports to a local work site because it is local, not because his organizational subunit headquarters are located there. Thus, while the members of the accounting department may have previously reported to a single fragmented location, these members may now report to one of several different locations, using telecommunications to perform those intraorganizational communications that were formerly done face-to-face. There are significant differences in transportation patterns resulting from these last two evolutionary steps. In the fragmentation process, there would be no effect or even possibly a detrimental effect on the average commuting distance for employees in a fragmented work site. Some employees would travel a shorter

141

distance to work at the new locations, but on the average it would be anticipated that the net result would be an increase in transportation to work. In the dispersed case, substantial reductions in transportation are anticipated since each employee now travels to the location closest to his residence.

The ultimate phase of this telecommunications–induced process is diffusion. In this case, an employee may not necessarily work for a single firm but may instead offer his particular services through a telecommunications–network to several different firms or clients. Thus, we have a telecommunications–induced return to the cottage industry. This particular phenomenon is beginning to appear in the form of remotely located secretarial services and is, of course, common among the professions. A significant tech–nological difference between the diffusion phase and the previous phases of the process is that a widespread capa–bility for switched data networks is required whereas in the previous stages the communications requirements could be satisfied by private data networks or leased line systems.

A SCENARIO

One technique used by the research group to both illustrate the telecommuting process and enable us to pinpoint technological considerations is the writing of a "scenario" which depicts a typical event in a segment of the information industry using telecommuting. As an example, I will summarize one of the scenarios we used, called "Secrepool".

142

The scene opens with our hero, Mr. Jim Nehring, sitting in his study at home, talking to the "Secrepool Distribution Center" on his telephone and arguing about their billing procedures. Having gotten the argument straightened out, Mr. Nehring hangs up and begins to record a letter on his tape recorder to one of the clients of the insurance company for which he works. In mid—message, he stops the tape, leaves the room, goes to the kitchen, and returns with a cup of coffee. He snaps the recorder on again and finishes the letter. At that point, he dials one of "Secrepool's" phone numbers, puts the phone head in its receptacle on his tape recorder, depresses several buttons on the phone carriage to indicate his identification and account number, starts the playback; and the letter is transferred to the "Secrepool" data bank.

The scene then shifts to another home where a small child is telling his mother, our heroine, that he does not feel well. His mother tests his warm forehead, advises him not to go to school, and puts him to bed in his room. She then walks to their family room, picks up a telephone hand set and dials a number. She sets the hand set on a recording device which is automatically activated by a signal transmitted through the telephone. She leaves the room and returns after squeezing some orange juice for her son. The recorder, in the meantime, had completed its reception of messages, had rewound the tape, and turned itself off.

She then puts on a head set, connected to the recorder and sits down in front of a computer terminal. As she types, the message appears on the screen above the keyboard. She

143

completes the letter and proofreads it. It is fine. She presses the "FILE" key of her keyboard; the letter disappears, its contents having been recorded on the tape cartridge attached to the terminal. After going through a series of these operations, she takes the filled cartridge out of the terminal, puts it in the recorder, dials the "Secrepool Distribution Center", and transfers her finished work to it.

The scene shifts again. Mr. Nehring now appears in his office the following day. He goes to his phone and dials a "Secrepool" number. He then identifies himself, turns on the recorder, and puts the phone head in its receptacle. Copies of his typed letter are taped on his recorder. When the tape is complete, he takes out the cartridge, puts it in the playback unit of his terminal, and the letter appears on the screen. Having read it through, he picks up an electronic pencil connected to the terminal, adds his signature, and presses the "MAIL" key. The letter is then sent by similar electronic means or by the postal system to its recipient elsewhere in the city or the country.

At each point in this scenario process, we can examine the conditions and see what kinds of technology are required to make it happen. We have done this for many other situations in the business world and discover one key fact. It is this: for most business purposes, at least those of a routine nature, the capabilities of present telephone type communications networks, augmented by graphical displays such as the one just shown, are adequate. The reason this is so important is that telephone type communications systems and their associated equipment are significantly less expensive than the video type of systems. A communications network which can handle only one television type signal has the capability for handling more than one thousand telephone type signals. With this consideration in mind, let us now return to an investigation of the dispersibility of the major national insurance company which we are studying.

SAMPLE CASES

As a first step in constructing a sample case, we plotted the current residential distribution of employees of the insurance company under study on a map of the Los Angeles area. We then postulated eighteen work centers as baseline locations for estimating the costs of telecommuting. Each of these centers corresponds to one of the centers of activity proposed by the Planning Department of the City of Los Angeles. Table 1 shows a typical set of data, developed under Dr. Frederic Carlson's direction, giving the dispersed commuting distances for the postulated network, the number of employees per center, and the estimated cost for installation of a private network interconnecting the dispersed centers. These network installation costs, when combined with operating costs for telecommuting, result in an annual telecommuting cost per employee of from $500 to $1000 per annum, depending on the details of the network design, amortization rates, etc. A critical factor in this cost analysis is the conclusion we have reached from evaluation

TABLE 1

BASELINE DISPERSED TELECOMMUTING NETWORK

Number of Nodes: 18

Distance of Nodes from Current Central Location:

>Minimum: 0.3 miles
>Maximum: 21.7 miles
>Average: 10.6 miles

Average Commuting Distance (one way):

>Current (single central location): 10.8 miles

>Dispersed

>>Node Maximum (55 employees): 11.5 miles
>>Node Minimum (121 employees): 1.1 miles
>>Average (1800 employees): 3.3 miles

Capital Cost of Private Network Installation:

>Cable Installation: $610,000
>Interface Computer Hardware: $2,175,000
>Terminals (one per employee): $10,215,000

Annual Amortized Cost Per Employee: $500

of the communications requirements of the insurance company, that almost all of the routine operations of the company can be performed using off—the—shelf computer, terminal, and telecommunications technology, with the communications system operating at audio bandwidths. The typical employee terminal is of the teletypewriter cum alphanumeric display variety.

The costs of commuting for the present work force of the insurance company have also been estimated and are shown in Table 2. Although the commuting mileage of the employees is known, it was assumed that their automobile purchasing habits were reasonably close to those of the national average figures, which were the ones used for the estimate. The table shows the marginal costs of commuting for two cases: the first in which the commuter uses the car solely for commuting and the second in which commuting use (assuming a single car household) only covers fifty percent of its total use. In the latter case, only those costs specifically attributable to commuting were used in the estimate to ensure conservatism. Here it can be seen that the annual commuting cost ranges from $650 to $1600. If we further refine the estimates by assuming a distribution of single and multiple car households, which is equivalent to the national average in metropolitan areas, and if we further assume that one car could be eliminated from each multi—car household inventory in favor of telecommuting, then we arrive at a gross annual average commuting cost of slightly under $1000. Thus, it can be seen that the direct costs of telecommuting for the cases studied compare favorably with those of commuting.

147

TABLE 2. Private Auto Commuting Direct Operating Costs

Cost Element	Average Annual Cost ($)			
	Commuter Use Only		50% Commuter Use*	
	Standard	Subcompact	Standard	Subcompact
Depreciation	643	302	not applicable	
Financing	166	99	not applicable	
Maintenance	315	260	158	130
Gasoline/Oil	260	145	252	138
Insurance	198	183	15(est.)	14(est.)
Parking	450	450	450	450
Taxes	75	45	not applicable	
TOTAL COSTS	2,173	1,538	875	732
Total Cost/Commuter**	1,671	1,183	673	563
Composite Cost/Commuter***	1,573		651	

---

*All of the figures shown are costs attributable solely to
 commuting. Costs which the owner would have to bear
 even if the use for commuting were discontinued (and
 ownership were continued) are not included.

**At 1.3 persons per automobile.

***Assuming 80% standard, 20% subcompact mix.

148

This consideration by itself is not expected to be sufficient to allow a clear decision in favor of telecommuting on the part of an information industry firm. For one thing, most such firms do not now pay the costs of commuting except indirectly through increased wages to central business district employees. Even where a wage/commuting influence factor is felt by the employer, the additional commuting cost burden assumed by the employer tends to be significantly less than the total commuting marginal costs. The costs of time lost in commuting are also not included. However, additional factors do play an important part in this decision. For example, the office space rent differential between the downtown facility of the insurance company studied and a typical dispersed site is comparable to the annual telecommuting costs. However, questions such as the increase or decrease of personnel productivity at the regional site remain to be established. Initial surveys of one small dispersed location recently set up by the insurance company indicate that both productivity and job satisfaction are higher at the dispersed site than at the central location. Further, many of the employees at the dispersed site have switched to the bicycle or walking as their form of commuting transportation. Those employees still using the private auto do so with a carpool. This remote site is a fragmented one, according to our evolutionary description, using conventional telephone lines and a daily courier system for their interorganizational communications.

TELECOMMUNICATIONS EFFECTIVENESS

As part of the USC research program, a survey has been made, directed by Dr. Gerhard Hanneman, of the attitudinal and motivational aspects of the uses of telecommunications for higher order information processes as typified by the Interactive Instructional Television System in operation at USC and at Stanford University. Both of these systems involve transmission of courses from the main campus to regional learning centers, using a standard television format with an audio return link from the centers to the main campus to allow students to ask questions of the instructors.

This lecture was originally taped in one of the USC Interactive Instructional Television classrooms. Four cameras are available for use in this process, all remotely controlled. One picks up a frontal view of me seated here or at the blackboard. One can get a side view of me or the class. One can pick up handwritten notes or large trans-parencies; and one can cover slides or movie films. This system is much more sophisticated than is required for the routine business activities I have been describing. However, it or some simpler version might be necessary for the performance of some of the higher order communi-cations functions of top level management. It might be inadequate for others.

In any case, if the participants in the Instructional TV classes were to commute to campus instead of taking their courses through the television system, their average round trip commuting distance would be seventeen miles, slightly below the national average commute—to—work distance. Since both the on—campus and remote students take the

150

same courses (the on—campus students viewing the lectures at the originating facility) and their performance in terms of grades earned has been essentially the same, we conclude that there is no appreciable loss in effectiveness produced by the telecommunications system. Furthermore, most of the remote participants were willing to pay a surcharge at least equivalent to their costs of transportation in order to telecommute to class.

IMPACT

Now that we have examined some of the basic concepts of telecommuting and covered some of the cost and effect—iveness issues, we are in a position to ask what all this means in terms of potential impact on future life. One major potential impact is in energy use.

The operating energy tradeoffs between telecommuting and private automobile commuting or even mass transit appear to be quite significant. We calculated the rela—tive energy consumption per commuter for the average employee of the insurance company we studied, using either the private auto, normally loaded mass transit, fully loaded mass transit, and telecommunications technology, respec—tively. The costs for each mode of transportation and for telecommunications were calculated in terms of equivalent kilowatt hours of primary fuel energy. That is, for the three transportation modes shown, the fuel energies were cal—culated directly. For the telecommunications case, we similarly calculated the fuel costs at a central electric power plant. This results in a number about three times higher than you would read on your power meter at home. If you have a well trained eye, you can see from the graph that the use of the private automobile costs about twenty-five times as much energy as telecommuting. That ratio decreases to about two—and—a—half times for fully loaded mass transit, a rare occurrence. Expansion of these figures on a national scale indicates that for each one percent of the urban commuter work force which substitutes telecommuting for commuting, assuming as we did before that telephone communications bandwidths are used, a net reduction of annual U.S. energy consumption of about fifteen billion kilowatt hours could result. These figures do not reflect the changes in energy use such as space heating, air conditioning, etc. which would result from the different urban structures and living patterns associated with tele-commuting, but do give an indication of the potential energy conservation attributes of telecommuting. They simultan-eously bring up the question of the impact of changing the form of delivered energy from gasoline to electricity, possibly exacerbating the problem of providing sufficient electrical power, even though a significant national energy saving could result.

Another area of potentially great impact is, of course, that of transportation systems. Since a major purpose of our study of telecommuting has been to see whether we could make material inroads on the twice—daily commuter rush, we see that the success of the telecommuting process could allow an urban structure in which our present highway systems are adequate for the job. Most urban mass transit systems now in planning are oriented around the problem of serving these two peak commuting loads every day. As a consequence they are designed primarily to funnel huge numbers of people to and from the central business districts of cities for these purposes and are consequently over-designed for the off peak hour loads. The same is true of our freeway systems. So the question becomes: Is mass transit obsolete? Our answer is no, but if telecommuting is successful, possibly mass transit systems should be designed differently. For example, since our model corporation is now dispersed into eighteen locations instead of one, where the people live three miles from work instead of ten, we can now envision localized mass transit systems which serve the residential areas around each urban node in this new conurbation on frequent and well-spaced schedules with less frequent service between nodes. Thus, people could still use mass transit systems to do shopping, attend cultural events and sports activities which might occur at other nodes around the city but would not be impeded by the lack of quality mass transit to perform their daily commute to and from work.

There may be significant impacts in land use planning and on the environment. We see here a set of conflicting forces for urban growth. Some of these are in favor of greater concentration of areas of the cities – the nodes – the others are for increasing urban sprawl. One researcher in this field, Dr. Peter Goldmark, is beginning to conduct experiments on the new rural community in which the in-habitants are fairly widely scattered around the countryside with low population densities, communicating with each other and with their work via various telecommunications

153

techniques. Our own research is concentrating more on the existing urban structure in an attempt to discover how it might evolve into some new form of community. We see as a likely step in this process what we are beginning to call the rural city in which we have mixes of both the familiar downtown business district area and suburban living. One major difference is that the future central business district will no longer be simply a business district; it will not be the antithesis of the bedroom community. Where tall buildings are now devoted solely to office use, new ones may evolve to a mixed selection of offices, living quarters, and entertainment facilities. Suburbanites may have the advantages of small town living in that they live and work in the same general area (and may actually even get to know their neighbors) while having the ability through telecommunications to enjoy the cultural activities of a major metropolis.

As with all cases of increasing freedom of choice, we begin to worry about the point where freedom becomes license. One of the clear potential results of the greater ability to relocate because of improved and cheaper tele-communications technology is that people will move to areas of great scenic beauty in such numbers as to destroy the resource they moved to be near. The choices are to risk the destruction of major natural scenic resources through inadequate planning for this possibility or to perform proper planning, restrict access to the resources, and provide alternate scenic areas in our existing cities. Interestingly enough, it seems possible that as people spend more time living in suburban areas, they may take more care in providing park lands in these areas, thus avoiding urban monotony, even where we may have urban sprawl.

The advent of telecommuting may provide some other economic opportunities other than the ones we have already discussed. One major possibility is an increasing ability to eliminate ghettos. One major factor contributing to the continuation of ghettos, at least in the Los Angeles area, is the inability of the ghetto resident to leave the area to find jobs elsewhere. Telecommuting would allow people to work without leaving the ghetto areas and would also afford the opportunity to perform on—the—job training, allowing the ghetto inhabitants to upgrade their capabilities to the point where they would be able to take jobs of in—creasing sophistication. The resulting influx of income could allow them to either upgrade the ghetto areas so that they are no longer ghettos, to move to other areas of the city, or more likely some combination of the two.

The impersonality of the telecommunications medium, as we have described it, is in some senses an inadvertent enforcer of equal opportunities. For normal working rela-tionships, the two people on either end of the telecommun-ications systems are unable to detect ethnic and racial differences. Work performed can be judged on objective bases without the tinge of biases of this nature. If, as we suspect, telecommuting, combined with some recently developed computer—assisted instructional techniques, can result in a net increase in variety of work offered to the individual worker, we can anticipate a perceptible increase in individual productivity as a result. The United States is where it is in the contemporary world because
155

it has been able to produce increasingly higher per capita productivity, not because its citizens have worked harder than the rest of the world.

There are also potential health and social effects of telecommuting. One major question is whether telecommuting will produce greater socialization or greater isolation. Will it produce apartness or togetherness? Our vision of the rural city mentioned before has a high togetherness component. But there are distinct possibilities of the reverse, if the man/machine interface is not properly designed. The key point is that care must be taken to ensure that telecommunications is used as a tool for greater human interaction rather than a wedge separating and isolating people.

There are some interesting physical health attributes to telecommuting. The most obvious of these is that if people start walking and cycling to work because the distance is reasonably short, they will get more exercise and will enjoy greater health, provided they are not run down by automobiles in increasing numbers. As people experiment more with the uses of communications technology as a consequence of telecommuting, we will have an increasing amount of remote health care delivery. We will then be able to complain that not only will physicians refuse to make house calls, but you may not even be able to see them at their offices. Much of the health care and diagnostic services can be accomplished via telecommunications, combined with appropriate medical services. Telecommuting may provide a new means for allowing the physically handicapped to once more become contributing

156

members of society. They will be able to work from their homes instead of vegetating there as they do now.

CONCLUDING REMARKS

These are some of the possibilities for the future which we have seen thus far. Although our research has not yet progressed to the point where we can clearly define the relative importance of these various impacts, we have been able to identify several areas of impact which appear to be of significant potential and importance. The results to date tend to indicate that the possibility of substituting telecommunications and computer technology for commuter transportation is a present reality which will be further enhanced as new technology is developed and new uses of the technology are made. It is important to point out that, although our research has concentrated on the uses of telecommunications technology solely as a transportation replacement for the performance of conventional and routine functions in the information industry, it allows the performance of new functions which have not been possible in many cases because of transportation restrictions, only a few of which have been enumerated here. No overnight miracles will happen, but a new set of desirable alternatives is appearing. All of these considerations point to the increasing importance of telecommunications and computer technology as influences on the course of future events. It further emphasizes the necessity for research toward anticipating these events and planning alternative futures.

11

ECONOMIC CONSTRAINTS ON THE NEW TECHNOLOGY

Maxwell E. McCombs

Television created a communication revolution in the United States. Within the mass media and throughout American life there were major changes, upheavals and reallocations. In 1947 television was brand new. Only 2.5% of American households had a set. Only a dozen years later, in 1959, 85.5% of American homes had television. No other mass medium saturated America so rapidly. In the process, radio was turned upside down, the movies were driven to the wall and entire new patterns of leisure behavior appeared in American homes.

Interest in professional sports soared. Television became the scapegoat for juvenile delinquency. Some even say television enabled John Kennedy to defeat Richard Nixon for the Presidency in 1960. The impact of television on American life is already part of our folklore.[1]

Like other aspects of mass communication, attention has centered on the effects of television. Little has been said about the social setting in which this new communication technology thrived. Where were the economic con—

straints on mass communication described by the Principle of Relative Constancy in the rapid—growth days of television? Were they simply inoperative? During the 12—year period from 1948 through 1959 when television was saturating the United States, consumers invested more than $10 billion in this new medium. This represents an average annual expenditure of about $800 million. Where did this money come from? What, if any, are the economic constraints on new communication technologies? What factors in the marketplace determine their success (in the case of TV) or failure (in the case of facsimile)? [2]

Consumers have three possible sources for money to spend on new communication media: new money in the economy, money now spent on other media and other non—media expenditures. How did each of these contribute to the successful financing of television in the United States?

The general economy was indeed growing during those years. Consequently, consumers did have more money to spend. In 1948, the average family had an income of about $5,000. This figure climbed steadily, and by 1959 it had reached $7,500, a 50% increase in 12 years. This "new money" represents one possible source of support for TV.

Of course, other media continued to operate during those years. After the advent of TV, some media continued to thrive financially in spite of new competition. But other media, particularly the movies, lost some of their business to TV. In 1948 when TV was still relatively new on the American market, motion picture admissions totaled $1.50 billion. Five years later, the movies' annual income had dropped to $1.17 billion, representing an annual net loss of $330 million. These dollars lost by the movie industry, and money lost by other media, might well have been a significant source of TV revenue. Indeed, since the decline of the movies is commonly attributed to television, one might turn this proposition around and assert that lost movie revenue in part financed television.

Dollars lost from some non—media sources also could have helped to finance TV. In 1949, for example, consumers spent $800 million less on jewelry, watches, houses and furniture than they had in 1947 before the advent of television.

Which of these three possible sources did, in fact, account for TV revenue from 1948 to 1959? Taking non-media sources first, if the Principle of Relative Constancy held between 1948 and 1959, no outside sources need have been tapped, and these non—media sources can be eliminated. According to this principle, consumers spend a relatively constant proportion of their income on media over the years. So, according to the principle, TV would not have brought about a significant increase in *total* media spending. Rather the money for television sets would have come from the unchanged, constant proportion of income spent on all media. Money shifting among the media together with general economic growth would sufficiently account for TV dollars in years of media constancy, and no outside sources need be tapped.

Did a condition of relative constancy exist for the years 1948—59 when TV was on the rise? The Principle of Relative Constancy has already been substantiated for the 40 years from 1929 through 1968. For the 12—year period in question here, the constancy principle was retested in four ways (Table 1). After determining the trend in consumer expenditures on media, this trend was analyzed, first controlling for fluctuations in personal income from year to year, and, second, controlling for changes in Gross National Product. Under both conditions, consumer spending on media was constant.

The third test for constancy examined the trend between 1948 and 1959 in consumer spending on media expressed as a percentage of total consumption spending. Here the trend is negative, not a constant pattern of spending. This even more strongly rejects non—media sources as a source of money to buy television sets. This would indicate that

TABLE 1

Trends in Consumer Spending on Media, 1948–1959

Dollars Spent by Consumers on Media Over Time,
Controlling for Average Personal Income [a]   .228
                                             (p=.250)

Dollars Spent by Consumers on Media Over Time,
Controlling for Gross National Product [a]   .344
                                             (p=.150)

Percent of Total Consumption Dollars Spent
by Consumers on Media Over Time   −.510

Percent of Income Spent by Consumers on Media
Over Time   −.658

[a] In constant dollars per household.

families did not cut other expenses to buy a TV set while maintaining previous levels of spending on mass media. All in all, the proportion of consumption spending going to mass media *declined* during the very period that television was growing. Finally, the trend in percentage of total personal income spent by consumers on mass media was examined. Here again a negative trend emerges. People were devoting less, not more, of their income to mass media.

On the basis of this evidence, we can eliminate the non—media category as a source of TV financing and turn to the two other categories to find the source of the TV dollars.

With regard to new money in the economy, did the economy actually grow enough during the years 1948—59 so that new money *could* have supplied all the TV dollars? A comparison of the percentage changes in media spending and in aggregate personal income over the 12—year period in Table 2 shows[3] that, except for 1949 and 1950, general economic expansion did exceed increases in consumer spending on media. In most years, the economy grew 10 to 20% faster than did media expenditures. Only in 1949 and 1950 did media spending grow faster than aggregate income, and the discrepancy between the two was less in those years than at any other time. Instead of income being ahead by its usual 10—20%, media spending did exceed income but only by 0.18% in 1949 and 6.67% in 1950. Although the magnitudes of these differences are small, there does seem to be some short—term dislocation of consumer spending on media in these two aberrant years. But these years are balanced out by other years, such as 1956 and

TABLE 2

*Increases in Media Dollars and Personal Income, 1948-1959
(Using 1947 Figures as a Base)*

	Media Dollars	Personal Income
1948	3.31%	9.84%
1949	9.55	8.74
1950	25.92	19.25
1951	25.73	34.03
1952	30.01	42.63
1953	36.84	50.61
1954	41.91	51.51
1955	47.95	62.19
1956	54.38	74.20
1957	61.79	83.90
1958	69.78	88.31
1959	84.79	100.91

TABLE 3

*Television Revenue and New Media Dollars, 1948-1959 (in Billions of
Actual Dollars, Using 1947 Figures as a Base)*

	Television Revenue	New Media Dollars
1948	$ .15	$ .17
1949	.47	.49
1950	1.12	1.33
1951	1.01	1.32
1952	1.02	1.54
1953	1.05	1.89
1954	.99	2.15
1955	.99	2.46
1956	.86	2.79
1957	.85	3.17
1958	.69	3.58
1959	.73	4.35

1957, when increases in media spending lagged far behind the growth of the economy.

Thus except in the two aberrant years 1949 and 1950 "new money" in the economy could have accounted for all increased spending on media. Did this in fact occur? Did the media actually take in enough new money to cover all TV dollars? Table 3 shows that the answer is an empirical "yes": in all years, the increase in the number of new dollars actually taken in by the media was enough to cover the increase in spending on TV sets entirely. Does this mean that those who claim TV prospered at the movies' expense are wrong? TV would not have needed any dollars lost by the movie industry if television set spending came solely from new money in the economy.

But other media, such as newspapers, magazines, sheet music, books and maps, also were consistently gaining revenue during these same years. Some of the new money must have gone to them, leaving an inadequate supply to cover TV. Thus the third source, losses from other media, must also have contributed to TV.

How did these two sources, new money and other media, combine to account for TV revenue? By definition:

$$A+B+C=D$$

where A = money lost from other media, B = money gained by other (non–TV) media, C = TV spending and D = new money in the economy going to mass media. In 1955, for example, the \$2.46 billion of new media money (D) is a result of \$.99 billion gained by TV (C), plus \$1.84 billion gained by the print media and non–TV audio–visual media (B), minus the \$.37 billion lost by movies (A). Our concern

164

now becomes: in what ways could *A, B* and *D* have combined to account for *C*?

There is an analogue here to the annual international balance of payments, a summary which obscures thousands of individual transactions. Here too, we have only yearly dollar figures and net change scores with which to work. We can never trace the exact path a dollar or individual consumer follows from year to year. We can, however, make certain assumptions about various combinations of factors which could have accounted for TV dollars and determine the empirical outcome of these assumptions.

First, let us suppose that all money lost by various media went directly to the other non—TV media which were gaining. What would then have been left for TV? (This assumption also implies that new money would have been the dominant source of TV revenue.)

Table 4 reveals that in every year, the actual dollar gains by non—TV media exceeded the losses. The gaining non—TV media would thus have absorbed all the money lost by other media (plus some of the ''new money''), and TV's sole source of money would have been new dollars in the economy. While this assumption is theoretically possible, it is intuitively implausible. The concept of functional equivalence is inconsistent with the details of the assumption as it empirically turns out. Movies, the dominant if not the sole medium involved in *A* over all 12 years, are not functionally equivalent to the dominant factors in *B*, newspapers and books. It seems inconceivable that people would take dollars from the movies (*A*) to invest more in print media (*B*). Thus we reject our first model

165

TABLE 4

Dollars Shifting Among Media, Television Revenue and New Media Dollars, 1948-1959 (in Billions of Actual Dollars, Using 1947 Figures as a Base)

	Give-ups (A)			Gains (B)		Television Revenue (C)	New Media Dollars (D)
	Print Media	Audio-Visuals[a]	Movie Admissions	Print Media	Audio-Visuals		
1948		.11	.09	.18	.03	.15	.17
1949		.21	.14	.30	.06	.47	.49
1950		.09	.22	.40	.14	1.12	1.33
1951		.18	.29	.57	.21	1.01	1.32
1952		.08	.36	.70	.25	1.02	1.54
1953			.42	.83	.43	1.05	1.89
1954			.38	.86	.70	.99	2.15
1955			.37	1.03	.83	.99	2.46
1956			.36	1.18	1.12	.86	2.79
1957			.47	1.46	1.34	.85	3.17
1958			.42	1.63	1.68	.69	3.58
1959			.32	1.88	2.05	.73	4.35

[a] Includes all audiovisuals except television and movies.

and proceed to a second, more plausible one.

Suppose that the money lost by the movie industry went directly to TV; that money lost by other media went to gains in non–TV media;[4] and that the remaining TV dollars were again supplied by new money. Functional equivalence supports the plausibility of this assumption: TV provides many of the same satisfactions that movies do, and Machlup considers them functional equivalents.[5] It is likely that consumers did indeed attend fewer movies as they started watching TV: the positive correlation between TV set sales and the decrease in movie ticket sales from 1948–59 ($r = +.62$) suggests equivalence and supports the plaus–ibility of our second assumption.

What pattern of support for TV follows from this assump–tion? In terms of actual dollars, while movies (A) would have provided a portion of TV revenue (C), new money (D) would also have been tapped to provide many TV dollars. For at least eight of the twelve years studied, new money accounts for two–thirds of the increase in TV set investment by consumers.

A better indicator can be obtained, however, when the actual dollars are corrected to constant dollars per house–hold, i.e. when controls for population and inflation are introduced. The purchasing power of the dollar in terms of 1957–1958 dollars fell over the twelve–year period from $1.19 in 1948 to $0.98 in 1957. In addition to this variation, a growing population could have further confounded the figures on media spending. From 1948 to 1959 the number of households jumped from 40 million to over 50 million. When our second model is analyzed in constant dollars per

167

household (Table 5), the dominant source of TV money shifts from new money to movie losses.

A possible third model is based on these assumptions: All money lost by other media went to TV. Money gained by other non—TV media would have come from new money, and any remaining new money would also have gone to TV. This assumes it is plausible to lump the other media losing money between 1948 and 1959 with movies as functional equivalents of TV.[6]

In terms of actual dollars, other media and new money contributed approximately equal portions to TV revenue. But again we have a better analysis of the assumption in terms of constant dollars per household. When we correct the figures for population and inflation, other media provide ample money to cover TV revenue, except in 1950, when they leave 16% of TV revenue to be supplied by new money.

To sum up, the Principle of Relative Constancy held during the twelve years that television saturated America. That is, the proportion of consumer money flowing to mass media remained fixed, and, despite significant economic growth—a 50% increase in personal incomes—TV's share of the consumer dollars was wrested away from other mass media, primarily the movies.[7]

Two conclusions can be drawn from this case study of TV, conclusions which may well apply to any communication medium trying to build an audience. First, the Principle of Relative Constancy is a valid description of audience spending behavior even when highly fascinating new media appear in the marketplace. Access to the public has a major economic constraint, in addition to the commonly

168

TABLE 16

Dollars Shifting Among Media, Television Revenue and New Media Dollars, 1948–1959 (in Constant Dollars per Household, Using 1947 Figures as a Base)

	Give-ups (A)			Gains (B)		Television Revenue (C)	New Media Dollars (D)
	Print Media	Audio-Visuals[a]	Movie Admissions	Print Media	Audio-Visuals		
1948	.76	8.82	8.06		.40	4.47	−12.43
1949		12.75	10.83	.92	1.11	13.22	− 8.31
1950	1.86	11.21	14.69	1.26	3.08	30.62	+ 8.66
1951	1.96	17.37	20.12	1.53	4.04	24.67	− 9.16
1952	.63	16.27	23.05	1.01	4.65	23.80	−10.23
1953		12.12	25.21	1.81	5.34	23.82	+ 6.32
1954		7.80	24.70	1.60	6.33	22.18	− 2.85
1955		7.10	26.96	4.37	7.03	21.87	+ 1.25
1956		3.42	25.69	5.42	8.14	18.21	+ 2.47
1957		2.36	29.23	8.10	8.76	17.00	+ 2.25
1958		.15	29.21	10.65	10.52	13.11	+ 2.96
1959			27.93	12.60	15.52	13.57	+12.80

[a] Includes all audiovisuals except television and movies.

169

discussed legal and technological constraints. Second, even in periods of rapid economic growth new media must battle some of the established media for a share of the market. It is unlikely that a new communication technology provides a totally new service. Rather such technologies are likely to be extensions of existing services. These functional equivalents must battle for economic survival or economic accomodation in the marketplace.

NEW COMMUNICATION TECHNOLOGY

Just as significant technological advances in electronics provided the groundwork for television, new electronic advances in the last decade have placed a host of new audio–visual communication devices in the realm of the technologically possible. Audio cassettes already are on the market. Video cassettes will be reaching the marketplace in the immediate future. Some speak of computers as a new mass medium. Others speak of cable television as a total alternative both to network commercial television and to the telephone system. Along with these projected networks of computer systems and ubiquitous cable TV are proposals for national satellite communication systems, either to facilitate existing forms of communication or to carry truly national mass communication that might even bypass the local relay between the source and the consumer. What implications does the Principle of Relative Constancy have for these new communication technologies? What economic constraints will influence whether the diffusion of these new media are as successful as television in the late 1940's and early 1950s or whether these technologies become the communication analogues of the Kaiser and the Edsel?

For some of these new technologies, there are legal as well as economic constraints on their success. Cable television and satellite systems may have their fate decided by the Federal Communications Commission, not by the consumer.

The audio cassette is essentially a simple change of packaging for the phonograph record. While the hardware required is different, an audio cassette or tape deck performs exactly the same service as the phonograph record. It does offer the relatively minor advantages of longer playing time and suitability for use in automobiles. Otherwise, cassettes and phonograph records are functionally equivalent. One would anticipate that changes in consumer spending would occur almost wholly within this narrow sphere of the mass communication market.

The video cassette, on the other hand, represents a significantly new set of alternatives for the consumer. Basically, the hardware using video cassettes (also variously called video cartridges and video discs) will convert the family TV into a kind of home movie projector and screen. Once this hardware is in place, the consumer can select from a plethora of available program cassettes. Everything now available on film and videotape can be repackaged. Some manufacturers promise the customer the option of recording his own cassettes from regular television programming, either for permanent archiving or simply for viewing at a more convenient time and then erasing it.[8]

But antecedent to any sweeping changes in communica-

171

tion service is the successful diffusion of the communication medium among the population. Money for new mass media must be taken away from older media and/or be created by economic growth. Since the consumer of video cassettes still must own an operating television set, spending cannot be cut here. The money must come from elsewhere.

Considering which of the media are functional equivalents of video cassettes, its primary competitors would seem to be movies, cable fees, recordings and live performances. Since the movies, particularly, suffered a severe setback with the initial introduction of television, it is reasonable to ask whether even a deathblow to the movie theatre would yield sufficient revenue to finance video cassettes as a mass medium.

Just as video cassettes could eliminate the local broadcaster in the distribution of programs, there is a similar potential in nationwide space satellite communication systems.[9] In 1971 the Federal Communications Commission began considering eight separate proposals. Since the various satellite proposals would require capital outlays of $40 million to $250 million, shifting existing communications traffic to a new system should insure its success.

While most of the communication satellite proposals focus on television network transmissions—a source of revenue estimated at $40 million annually if one system gets the entire business—the Hughes Aircraft Company proposal envisions a new communication service aimed directly at the consumer in the marketplace. Hughes proposes to distribute at least a dozen simultaneous programs to cable TV systems (CATV) throughout the country. On its

172

dozen channels, Hughes is considering offering all—news, all—sports, all—science and all—public affairs stations. Since many CATV systems have a capacity of 20 to 40 channels, this kind of satellite communication distribution system would help utilize this capacity and add a measure of diversity to existing television.

Obviously, a major factor in the success of this proposal is the successful diffusion of CATV and the creation of demand for the variety of audio—visual services planned by Hughes. Here the Principle of Relative Constancy again describes a key constraint. CATV and the program services it offers must compete with existing open—circuit TV, with the movies, with video cassettes and perhaps with other communication technologies waiting in the wings.

While the ultimate fate of CATV also may be decided by the FCC, not the marketplace, CATV has already begun to diffuse across the country.[10] In 1971 there were about 2500 CATV operations serving 4500 communities and viewed by approximately 15 million people daily at an annual consumer outlay of $300 million. That is still a small fraction of the aggregate consumer spending on all broad—casting, but the growth rate is about 20% annually and CATV is beginning to move from the rural, isolated regions where it was born into the big cities.

CATV moves television further away from mass commun—ication. Its 20— to 40—channel capacity fragments the mass audience. As the president of TelePrompTer Corporation, the largest CATV operator, has remarked, "Commercial television is in the scarcity business." With only 24 hours in the day and with the ability to broadcast only one program at a time, the commercial broadcaster is highly constrained in the programming he can offer and the amount of advertising he can sell. CATV is not in the scarcity business and can offer a greater variety of programming. [11]

But CATV will not necessarily sell more advertising. There are two reasons for this. First, CATV's multiple channel capacity fragments the audience so there are fewer viewers per program to market to the advertiser. Second, since each viewer pays directly for watching CATV–$5 a month in the case of TelePrompTer–advertising income is less essential.

Furthermore, a variety of income sources other than television programs are envisioned for CATV. Some predict CATV will become a two–way communication system, a viable alternative to the telephone and postal systems handling most of our business and personal messages. Others see CATV as a common carrier, that is, a physical facility to be used by consumers to carry whatever information or entertainment they desire. This point of view envisions the creation of large information storage and retrieval systems where films, TV shows, reference materials, perhaps even complete news services are available on call. CATV would be the medium linking individuals to these vast data banks, enabling each household to print its own newspapers, books and magazines. Mass communicators would continue to produce programs and news copy, but this work would not be disseminated in its present forms. Rather it would be "warehoused" in computer systems to which the public has access through CATV. If a particular program or piece of information was desired, the consumer would call for

174

it. Each consumer could become his own programming director and news editor if he desired. Perhaps there will even be audio/visual town meetings and individually pro—duced programs offered to whomever is interested.[12] The future promises a whole new realm of communication exper—iences and services—*if* consumer support is available to establish them in the marketplace.[13]

While these new technologies promise amazing new individual communication services, they are very costly. Technically, a CATV system with a host of auxiliary gadgets could create a versatile home communication center. This center would supplant—tremendously exceed—the present services of newspapers, movies, television, the post office, telephone and many other communication media. But the estimated cost for a million such consoles in American homes is $250 per month for each console.[14] That is almost as much a month as consumers now spend in an entire year on mass communication. In 1968 consumers directly spent an average of $278.60 per household on mass communication. Advertisers spent a little more that year per household—$296.64—for a total annual expenditure of $575.24 per house—hold on mass media. Even if the costs of telephone and postal services are added on to that total, we would still account for no more than four or five months rental on a home communication center. To succeed in the marketplace with a monthly fee of $250 would require that the home communication center must displace most of the existing communication services now in the marketplace. The Prin—ciple of Relative Constancy could no longer hold and there would not be enough money available to pay the bills. More

175

likely, the advent of the home communication center depends on technological advances that will lower the cost. A cheaper price makes the odds more favorable for a successful competitive struggle with existing media and communication services.

All our previous experience in mass communication suggests that new media must battle the established channels of communication for a foothold in the marketplace. Even when exciting and fascinating new mass media have appeared in the past the Principle of Relative Constancy has held. With the constraint described by that principle operating, a struggle between the new media and those already in the marketplace is inevitable. The decline of the newspaper dates from the appearance of the movie. Decades later the movies were battered in turn by the appearance of television. But the new media do not always succeed in wresting part of the market away from the older media. FM radio still remains a marginal mass medium; facsimile never made it at all. In calculating the odds on all the communication technologies now on the horizon actually becoming mass communication services, the economic constraint in the marketplace is a key factor.

---

1. See Sidney Kraus, ed., *The Great Debates* (Bloomington: Indiana University Press, 1962); Joseph T. Klapper, *The Effects of Mass Communication* (Glencoe: The Free Press, 1960); Leo Bogart, *The Age of Television* (New York: Frederick Ungar Publishing Co., 1956).

176

2. Mary A. Koehler, "Facsimile Newspapers: Foolishness or Foresight?," *Journalism Quarterly*, 46:29–36 (1969).

3. In choosing the base for computing this and subsequent tables, several problems were considered. First, there is the problem of the discontinuity of TV investments by consumers. The same people are likely to attend movies, and resubscribe to newspapers and magazines year after year, but the people who buy TV sets this year are probably not the same ones who bought TV sets last year. Does the fact that TV investments are made by largely differing populations of consumers from year to year make TV figures less comparable to investments in other media, which are made by largely continuous consumer populations? It was decided that our interests here concern total annual investments and net changes in the various media and are independent of the individuals who are doing the investing. Regardless of whether it comes from the same or different consumer, the total number of dollars spent annually on each of the media are directly comparable.

Secondly, what base should be used in computing change figures? Should 1947 figures be used as a fixed base, or should changes be calculated with a floating base, from year to year? It was decided that a fixed 1947 base would be preferable, largely to avoid having to ignore certain years because of negative numbers which would result if a floating base were used. Table 4, for example, when calculated using a floating base, yields 7 unuseable years: TV dollars were negative in 1951, 1952 and 1954–58; therefore it would not make sense to look for any source of TV revenue in those years, and we are left with only

177

5 out of 12 useable years. Since this problem arose in Tables 1, 3, and 4, all the tables were calculated using 1947 as a fixed base to achieve maximum consistency.

4. Several pieces of evidence suggesting a lack of impact by television on newspaper circulation are reported by Harvey J. Levin, "Competition Among Mass Media and the Public Interest," *Public Opinion Quarterly*, 18 (1954). pp. 73–4.

5. Fritz Machlup, *The Production and Distribution of Knowledge in the United States* (Princeton: Princeton University Press, 1962), pp. 246–7.

6. See Table I in Appendix A; also Machlup, *ibid.*, Table VI–14 and p. 225.

7. For a detailed case study of television's impact on the movies and other mass media see Paul T. Scott, "The Mass Media in Los Angeles Since the Rise of Television," *Journalism Quarterly*, 31:161–66, 192 (1954).

8. Hollis Alpert, "The Cassette Man Cometh" and Ivan Berger, "Someday Morning for the Culture Cans," *Saturday Review*, 54, No. 5: 42–47, 60 (January 30, 1971).

9. Wilbur Schramm, *Communication Satellites for Education, Science and Culture*. (Paris: UNESCO, 1968, Reports and Papers on Mass Communication, No. 53).

10. Ralph Lee Smith, "The Wired Nation," *The Nation*, 210:582–606 (May 18, 1970). Also, H. J. Barnett and E. Greenberg, "On the Economics of Wired City Television," *American Economic Review*, 58:503–8 (1968).

11. William J. Slattery, "Do You Know What's Going to Happen to Cable TV?," *TV Guide*, Vol. 19, No. 14 (April 3, 1971).

12. William C. Woods, "When the Boob on the Tube Is You," *Washington Post*, April 30, 1971, B—1.

13. Ben H. Bagdikian, *The Information Machines: Their Impact on Men and the Media* (New York: Harper and Row, 1970).

14. Bruce M. Owen, "Public Policy and Emerging Technology in the Media," Studies in the Economies of Mass Communication, Memorandum No. 92 (Research Center in Economic Growth, Stanford University, November 1969), pp. 8—9.

THE FATE OF EXISTING MEDIA

While all the new communication technologies and services joust for a place in the marketplace, what is the fate
of existing communications media? The constraint described
by the Principle of Relative Constancy implies that significant shifts will occur in the older media. Usually it will
be a mixture of decline and reconstructing. The movies, and
to some extent the newspaper, already reflect this. Both
have suffered some decline in the relative popularity of their
service. Both have modified their mass communication product and both exhibit some organizational changes.

At the far edge of the established media marketplace
lie the fine arts. "The arts cannot live on what the market
can offer." [1] They never really have and are less likely
to with increasing competition from new communication
media. In short, survival of the fine arts may depend entirely
on the willingness to subsidize this communication service
from public funds. There have been numerous demands
in recent years to do exactly this, recognition that the money
in the marketplace is insufficient and that donations from
private patrons and foundations are too erratic to support
a sustained communication system of fine arts.

Just short of actual appropriations from public funds to
support some communication medium is the use of government
power to intervene in the marketplace and establish conditions under which the medium can survive economically.
Generally, this means limiting the competition. This is precisely what the major movie producers attempted to do through
the courts in 1970. Charging that two television networks,
CBS and ABC, had violated the anti-trust laws, seven major

180

movie producers sought a permanent injunction barring them both from film production and also from filming television programs. For an industry that has been in decline—both absolutely and relatively—since 1946 this attempt at manipulation of the marketplace by means of the legal system represents a last ditch defense. The only major studio not participating in the suit was Twentieth Century Fox. The next year leaders of the motion picture industry met with President Nixon to plead for special tax relief for their industry. The importance of these efforts are underscored by the trends in movie expenditures by consumers over the past twenty—five years and by the looming competition for movies from the new audiovisual communication technologies. These are *last ditch* efforts because the movie industry already has passed through the traditional economic solutions to overwhelming competition. Many of the famous studios of the past no longer exist. They long ago darkened their stages and went out of business. Other studios survived through merger, either with other movie producers or with non—media enterprises able to back them financially. Two of the biggest Hollywood studios, Warner Bros. and Columbia Pictures, consolidated their physical plants while maintaining separate production and business operations. The precedent for this kind of merger is, of course, found in the joint—operating agreements of the daily newspaper business.

NEWSPAPER RETRENCHMENT

For decades there has been considerable concern over the decreasing number of American dailies, especially the decreasing number of competing dailies.[2] While some attribute this trend to monopolistic and anticompetitive business practices by newspaper publishers seeking higher profits,[3] examination of newspaper trends in light of the Principle of Relative Constancy offsets many of the arguments advanced to prove the anticompetition thesis.

The high water mark for the total number of daily newspapers in the United States was reached in 1909–10.[4] At that time there were 2,202 daily newspapers in the United States. The number of daily newspapers steadily declined after that, although there is some indication of a leveling off at about 1,750 in recent years. This peak year for the number of newspapers, 1909–10, coincides closely with the rise of the movie as a new mass communication medium. As the movie began to make rapid gains in the marketplace, as the consumer began to shift some of his media dollars, it is plausible, according to the Principle of Relative Constancy, to find a decline in the number of daily newspapers able to exist in the marketplace.

Looking more specifically at the lack of competition among newspapers—a situation true for 97% of the United States' 1500 daily newspaper cities in 1968—this is a trend that has been running since 1880. In that year 38.6% of the American cities with daily newspapers had no newspaper competition. By 1920 it was over half (57.4%) and by 1930, it had passed the three–quarters mark (79.4%). This trend

182

suggests that the combination of rising costs,[5] limited consumer and advertiser spending on media,[6] and competition from new communication media have resulted in fewer newspapers.[7]

Newspaper circulation per household also peaked and began to decline as the movie established itself in the marketplace. Less than a decade after the highwater mark for total number of producing units, circulation per household hit a peak of 1.38 copies per household and began a slow decline that is still continuing.[8]

The fact that locally competing newspapers virtually have disappeared from all except the largest cities has led even a former attorney for the Antitrust Subcommittee of the U.S. Senate to admit that there seems to be an 'economic spectrum' which limits the number of papers the country can support, just as there is a physical spectrum which limits the number of broadcasting stations.[9]

The behavior pattern described by the Principle of Relative Constancy is a key determinant of this "economic spectrum." Because of the limited amount of money available to support *all* mass communication, the present pattern is for a single daily in cities up to approximately 150,000 population; one morning and one evening paper under single ownership (or in joint operating arrangements) in cities from 150,000 to 650,000; and two or more competing dailies only in cities of over 650,000. In short, economic constraints on mass media in the marketplace suggest that the observed disappearance through merger and suspension of dozens of daily newspapers was economically inevitable. Or, as Nixon put it: ". . . *the natural working of economic*

183

laws is almost entirely responsible for the trend toward the elimination of local newspaper competition."[10]

Of course, in 88% of the cities in which a daily newspaper operates without competition from other newspapers it does have competition from broadcast media.[11] As radio and TV entered the mass communication market, the economic pie was resliced to include their share. As the Principle of Relative Constancy predicts, the result is a smaller slice for daily newspapers. As costs continue to increase, more newspapers may disappear from the market. Given the constraint of relative constancy, only so much of the increase in operating costs can be passed on to advertisers and consumers. Put another way, the existence of a newspaper—or any mass medium—depends on two questions: 1) how much does it cost to operate? and 2) given the constraint described by the Principle of Relative Constancy and the existence of other media in the same market, is enough money available to meet these operating costs? In many communities the threshold of profitable—or even break—even—operation for two competing newspapers is far above the level of economic support that actually is available. In some communities not enough money is available to support even a single newspaper.

Efforts to start new newspapers have frequently overlooked the economic facts of life described by the Principle of Relative Constancy. To compete against an established newspaper it is clearly necessary to offer a strong editorial product. But, as attempts in Atlanta and several other cities demonstrate, even where the new paper offers an attractive alternative editorial viewpoint, this is not enough to insure

184

success.[12] A popular, appealing editorial package is a necessary, but not sufficient, condition for survival in the mass communication marketplace; the market must be large enough to provide sufficient money to support competing newspapers. As the success of urban community newspapers —the suburban shoppers among them—demonstrate,[13] it is necessary to consider both the social function and economics of a mass medium.[14]

This is not the place to pursue all the implications of these economic patterns for antitrust litigation. However, the economic situation outlined by the Principle of Relative Constancy becomes the key to antitrust suits against so-called *failing businesses*. This refers to the legal doctrine which holds that the acquisition of a company by a competitor does not violate the antitrust laws if the firm taken over is in grave danger of bankruptcy. In the landmark Tucson case (U.S. vs Citizen Publishing Co.) the Justice Department antitrust division attacked the legality of joint operating agreements. Under a joint operating agreement two competing newspapers in a single city combine their printing, advertising, circulation and business operations while the news and editorial operations of the two newspapers remain separate and independent. Since one newspaper appears in the morning and the other in the afternoon, the sharing of printing and business facilities is feasible and results in marked economies. The major argument advanced by the defense for the Tucson newspapers was that joint operating agreements are necessary for the economic survival of two independent newspapers in many cities. Twenty—two cities have such arrangements. But in the

Tucson case the Supreme Court did not see the danger of economic demise and rejected the failing—company doctrine.[15] The Principle of Relative Constancy suggests the inevitability of some mergers or joint operating agreements. But, of course, evaluations and decisions must be made on a case—by—case basis.

TELEVISION

Just as television dislocated the older media, especially radio and the movies, it in turn is being confronted by the new technology. With cable TV and cassettes on the horizon, there are predictions that at least one network will be forced out of prime time—or that another may turn exclusively to news and sports. As yet these are only speculations. But by 1971 cigarette advertising was off the air and coupled with a slowed down economy, the golden days of TV appeared to be over.

Michael Dann, who guided CBS's programming strategy at the height of its dominance of the ratings, believes "it would be a grave mistake to assume that a healthy economy would return the networks to the profit levels of 1969. Those days will never return any more than the movies will ever again enjoy the profits of the 1930's." Dann was referring to the 1970 decline in television network revenues, the television industry's first. Until then, each year had surpassed the previous year. "By the time we enter into the wired—home society, probably by 1980, I think the service will be so fragmentized with 40 channels going into the home that the long run looks far more serious than the short

186

run. Network service as we've known it cannot exist."[16] The economic factors affecting television in the early 1970s— a slowing economy and the loss of a major segment of advertising—may be short lived. But the long run promised a major confrontation in the marketplace,[17] a confrontation whose outcome is shadowed by the economic constraints of the mass media marketplace.

---

1. Fritz Machlup, *The Production and Distribution of Knowledge in the United States* (Princeton: Princeton University Press, 1962), p. 224. Also see W. J. Baumol and W. G. Bowen, "On the Performing Arts: The Anatomy of Their Economic Problems," *American Economic Review, 55:495–502 (1965).*

2. Raymond B. Nixon, "Implications of the Decreasing Numbers of Competitive Newspapers." In Wilbur Schramm, ed., *Communications in Modern Society* (Urbana: University of Illinois Press, 1948). Also, Nixon, "Trends in Daily Newspaper Ownership Since 1945," *Journalism Quarterly,* 31:161–66, 192 (1954); "Local Monopoly in the Daily Newspaper Industry," *Yale Law Journal,* 61:948–1009 (1952); Nixon and Jean Ward, "Trends in Newspaper Ownership and Inter–Media Competition," *Journalism Quarterly,* 38:3–14 (1961).

3. Keith Roberts, "Antitrust Problems in the Newspaper Industry," *Harvard Law Review,* 82:319–66 (1968).

4. Raymond B. Nixon, "Trends in U.S. Newspaper Ownership: Concentration with Competition," *Gazette,* 14:181–93 (1968).

5. Detailed statistical data are found in Richard E. Chapin, *Mass Communications* (East Lansing: Michigan State University Press, 1957), p. 12 and Tables 10—12. See also Charles V. Kinter, "Economic Problems in Private Ownership of Communications," in Schramm (1948), *op. cit.;* James E. Pollard, "Spiraling Newspaper Costs Outrun Revenues 1939—1949," *Journalism Quarterly,* 26:270—76 (1949); Leslie McClure, "Mounting Production Costs: The Newspaper's Dilemma," *Journalism Quarterly,* 31:304—10 (1954).

6. The parallel trends in consumer and advertiser spending on mass media are reported above.

7. Royal H. Ray, "Economic Forces as Factors in Daily Newspaper Concentration," *Journalism Quarterly,* 29:31—42 (1952); Paul Block Jr., "Facing Up to the 'Monopoly' Charge," *Nieman Reports,* 9:3—7 (1955); Milburn P. Akers, "Chicago's Newspaper Concentration," *Nieman Reports,* 13:21 (July 1959).

8. Melvin L. DeFleur, *Theories of Mass Communication* (New York: David McKay Company, 1970), p. 20.

9. Nixon (1968) *op. cit.,* p. 185.

10. Raymond B. Nixon, "Who Will Own the Press in 1975?," *Journalism Quarterly,* 32 (1955), p. 14, italics supplied.

11. Guido H. Stempel, "A New Analysis of Monopoly and Competition," *Columbia Journalism Review,* 6:11—12 (1967).

12. Frank Veale, *The Atlanta Times Inside Story* (Greenville, Ga.: Gresham Printing Co., 1965); John M. Harrison, "The End at Lima," *Columbia Journalism Review,* 3:58—9

188

(1964), and "Post—Mortem: Too Late for Lima," *Columbia Journalism Review*, 5:38 (1966); Lewis Donohew, "PM: An Anniversary Assessment," *Columbia Journalism Review*, 4:33—6 (1965).

13. Morris Janowitz, *The Community Press in an Urban Settling* (Glencoe: The Free Press, 1952), pp. 46—52.

14. George Fox Mott, *et al.*, *New Survey of Journalism*, Fourth Edition Revised (New York: Barnes & Noble, 1958), Chapter 40; Poynter McEvoy, "The Reader Needs a Ten Cent Newspaper—Here's Why—The ABC of Newspaper Economics," *Nieman Reports*, 8, July 1954, 3—8; *Yale Law Journal*, "Local Monopoly in the Daily Newspaper Industry," Vol. 61, No. 6, p. 959.

15. For additional discussion of the legal implications in this case, see Harold L. Nelson and Dwight L. Teeter Jr., *Law of Mass Communications* (Mineola, N.Y.: The Foundation Press, 1969), pp. 500—504; and Donald M. Gillmor and James A. Barron, *Mass Communication Law* (St. Paul: West Publishing Co., 1969), pp. 556—66.

16. Jerry Buck, "TV Industry in Midst of Upheaval," Associated Press. (Durham *Morning Herald*, March 14, 1971, p. 7D.)

17. "What's Ahead for Television," *Newsweek*, 77:72—79 (May 31, 1971).

THE END OF MASS COMMUNICATION

Many of the current technological barriers to information—seeking and divertissement—seeking should dissolve with the advent of the new communication media. Video cassettes, cable television and computerized home communication centers each promise that a wealth of material now packaged for disparate media will become available in a single medium that is receiver—controlled. Prime time can be individually determined. It will depend on the schedule of each individual and when he wishes to use mass communication.

Mass communication will no longer mean the simultaneous diffusion of identical messages to mass audiences. There will still be mass production of identical massages: on the production end, there may be little change except in packaging. But on the receiving end there may be a true revolution in human behavior. The mass audience—millions of people simultaneously (or, nearly simultaneously) receiving identical messages—may well become a thing of the past. Each individual can structure his own individual "mass" communication. From the audience viewpoint, what was

190

mass communication may become a more personal and individual thing.

In line with this possibility we already have seen many of the mass circulation magazines disappear. Specialty magazines with relatively small audiences dominate the industry in terms of proportion of total magazine circulation. Similarly, the traditional strength of the newspaper has been its ability to satisfy the specialized needs of thousands of individuals with a single daily product. Increasing fragment-ation and individualization of mass communication has numerous behavioral implications. Toffler argues that one of these new communication technologies, video cassettes, will quicken the pace of change in American life, moving us away from national conformity and standardization in the arts and popular culture.[1] Marshall McLuhan also predicts that video cassettes will influence "every aspect of our lives—will give us new needs, goals, and desires, and will upset all political, educational and commercial establish-ments."[2] Similar predictions might be made for the other new communication technologies which expand the flexibility and scope of communication.

But this fundamental change in the nature of the "mass media" is subject to very severe economic constraints. All our experience over the past four decades substantiates the Principle of Relative Constancy. Only a small and fixed proportion of the economy is available to finance mass communication. Over the years the pie has grown, but at the same rate as the economy which produced the pie was grow-ing. New media in the marketplace did not produce a bigger pie; instead, the old pie was resliced to feed the newcomer.

191

Some of the new communication technologies now on the horizon require such large dollar support, such a large slice of the pie, that they must drastically reduce the share of several existing competitors if they are to survive in the marketplace.

Not only do the older mass media tend to shrink—relatively, if not absolutely—with the advent of new communications technologies; it may be that eventually all real media growth will come to a halt. Over past decades the amount of mass communication—and mass media hardware—acquired by the average American has grown fantastically, as have personal incomes. Homes now are a clutter of TV and radio sets, stereos, newspapers, magazines and other artifacts of mass communication. The clutter is not likely to disappear, but it may stop growing despite continued economic growth.

Economic growth has brought a proliferation of goods, gadgets and services. The consumption of these, Staffan Linder observes in *The Harried Leisure Class*, costs time.[3] As consumption continues to increase—time may become increasingly scarce.

The clearest examples of pleasure that are on the increase will be found among activities based on the use of things. The average income elasticity of such pursuits will be high. The environment of the typical consumer is a dense jungle of things: a house and a summer cottage; cars and a boat; TV, radio and a record player; records, books, newspapers, and magazines; clothes and sport clothes; tennis racket, badminton racket, . . . It is the total time spent in using all these things that increases; simultaneously, however, the time allocated to each of them individually is declining. [4]

For a time the consumer can increase the amount or number of goods enjoyed per time unit. He sips his martini, scans his newspaper and listens to the stereo simultaneously. But there must be some limit. Indeed, signs of the limit already are appearing. We are already in the age of half—read and unread magazines. Americans also seem less eager to acquire so many new machines, whether it be a car every year or the latest wrinkle. If indeed the goals or needs of each consumer are fixed, a voluntary consumption maximum eventually has to be reached. As incomes grow, more and more wants will be gratified. Ultimately, the the utility of additions to income and, especially consumption, will be zero. It can be argued, of course, that the tremendous growth of mass communication—growth perhaps constrained only by the consumer's ability to finance it—refutes this notion of fixed wants.

At least so far in our economic history consumers have continued to want more and more. The scope of consumer demand has increased along with income. [5] But even if our needs are infinite and production techniques continue to improve, there is a further possibility of the scope for continued consumption increases becoming exhausted.... The limit need not be set by our resources on the production side or by needs on the consumption side. The decisive factor can instead be a resource on the consumption side, namely time. [6]

The Principle of Relative Constancy describes a major economic constraint on the growth of media in the market—

place over at least the past 40 years. But even with continued economic growth, mass media consumption may reach
asymptote, with the ultimate constraint likely to be scarcity
of time. For the immediate decades ahead, these two factors—
time and money—will jointly constrain the growth of mass
media in the marketplace.

---

[1] Alvin Toffler, *Future Shock* (New York: Random House,
1970).

[2] Quoted in *Time*, August 10, 1970, p. 40.

[3] Staffan B. Linder, *The Harried Leisure Class* (New York:
Columbia University Press, 1970).

[4] *Ibid*, p. 90.

[5] George Katona, *The Mass Consumption Society* (New
York: McGraw—Hill, 1964).

[6] Linder, *op. cit.*, p. 125.

12

THE IMPACT OF COMMUNICATION TECHNOLOGY: PROMISES AND PROSPECTS

Natan Katzman

New communication technologies do not automatically solve—and may aggravate—social problems because of unequal use. An examination of the evidence and a discussion of the deepening dilemma.

Changes in man's ability to communicate over time and space result from innovations in both technology and methods of using technology. The development of new materials or devices, such as papyrus and communication satellites, has profoundly affected human communication. The ability to communicate is also changed as a result of new uses of materials and devices that are already available. Phonetic alphabets, mass—circulation journalism, and the introduction of television into schools are examples. After 100 years of accelerating changes in our ability to transmit and store information (the telephone had not been perfected in 1875, and high—speed printing on cheap paper was only beginning to make a major impact), new and still uninvented techniques,

195

from computer—aided instruction to home—printed newspapers (1), have the potential to produce drastic changes in western society. The adoption of already common (to us) communication techniques and technologies [1] by people in developing nations may cause even more severe changes.

With extraordinary frequency we are presented with the "promise" of new media and new ways of using currently available hardware. The future is often portrayed as a technological wonderland in which communication techniques have cheaply and painlessly solved major social, economic and educational problems. An examination of history, current information, and the logic of the situation reveals less optimistic expectations. [2]

Communication policy is a significant factor in the future shape of social systems. Certain phenomena seem to recur as new communication techniques and technologies are introduced, and it seems important to study these patterns in order to formulate effective policies. My central concern is with the relationships between new communication techniques and the distribution of *information* [3] in society. I shall present six propositions about these relationships, note some evidence, and discuss the major implications.

Proposition 1: Adoption of new communication techniques and technologies tends to increase the amount of information transmitted and received by individuals in a society.

There is a relationship between communication technologies which are adopted and the information transmitted and received by an "average" individual.[4] If this proposition is valid, the adoption of a new communication technique or technology should be expected to raise the overall level of material distributed by mass media, raise the overall level of of skill and knowledge of users of mass media and information systems, or increase the amount of communication passing through interpersonal channels. Although new technological developments may reduce the impact of prior technologies, *the net effect of innovation tends to be a net increase in information available* and acquired at all channels. Thus the printing press may have put an end to the wandering minstrel, television may have destroyed the general–circulation magazine, and the new technologies of information storage and retrieval may make library buildings anachronisms. Despite their intrusion into traditional modes of communication, such changes seem to result in an overall information gain.

Naturally there are limits to the generality of this premise. New technology is not introduced in a vacuum; the costs, skills, channel capacity, and political considerations associated with an innovation all influence the degree to which it will change the communication patterns of individuals.

Unless a culture and its artifacts are totally destroyed, the absolute number of things known by that culture cannot decline if there are media to preserve knowledge. However, I am proposing that the total amount of information transmitted and received by *individuals* will increase. This implies that there will be an increase in the number of *hubits* [5] of information distributed among people, not just in a growing number of *bits* available to a culture.

Proposition 2: All individuals receive more information after the adoption of a new communication technology.

The effects of changing communication technique and technology *eventually reach all individuals* and provide an increment in the amount of information they receive. In some cases, new communication methods directly provide new information to individuals. For other people this increment may occur as the result of a multi—stage flow. (Thus, illiterate individuals receive more information from literates, who receive more from advanced print technology.) The degree of impact and the distribution of impact depend on the variables associated with the technology: resource and skill requirements, channel capacity, political considerations, and relative advantage. Some new technologies will have more universal direct effects than others. (Radio, for example, does not require literacy or great resources of the listener.) Other innovations—such as computerized retrieval systems—may provide most individuals with increased information via a multi—step flow through other people.

Proposition 3: With the adoption of a new communication technology, people who already have high levels of information and ability will gain more than people with lower initial levels.

This premise describes an empirical phenomenon which seems to be almost universal. The effect of the adoption of a new technique becomes twofold. On the one hand, it raises the information level of all individuals; and on the other hand, it widens the gap between the "information—rich" and the "information—poor" in society.[6] New communication techniques and technologies give information gains to individuals as a monotonic function of initial information levels. The range of levels (and the gap between multimodal groups) widens as a result.

The effect is found in studies of various innovations—most especially in the application of technology to developing nations, but also in the introduction of new techniques within advanced systems such as U.S. universities. Rogers (12, p. 332) proposes that "new ideas may tend to make the rich richer and the poor poorer." His statement refers to the effects of any innovation on the finances of people in developing nations, but it may be applied just as well to the information levels of any people faced with new communication techniques or technology.

There are several reasons for the effect:

1. *People who first learn of or adopt an innovation are different from those who find out or adopt later.* They tend to have more education, higher status, more exposure to mass media, better use of interpersonal channels, more social participation, a more cosmopolite nature, and a higher level of literacy (12, p. 107). Thus, the first impact of new communication techniques or technologies is upon subgroups which are already more likely to communicate and have information than subgroups which adopt the changes at a

later date.

2. *The same message transmitted through a communication channel presents more bits of information to people with lower initial levels of information* than it does to people with higher initial information levels. Here, the receiver—oriented definition of information is useful. A relatively unexpected message requires greater change of the receiver. If too much change is required, the message may be ignored or mis—understood; the net effect will be that no information is transmitted. "Boil water to kill germs and avoid disease" is a more complex message to those who do not already know germ—disease theory. When new techniques are used to transmit any message more efficiently, people who do not have sufficient background fall behind those who have relevant prior knowledge.

3. *There is an uneven initial distribution of financial resources.* People with more money are in a position to acquire new and better technology more readily than people with less money. Wealthier school districts are most able to purchase media for computer—aided or other advanced tech—niques of instruction. Poorer districts, that cannot afford such technology, fall behind.[7] People with money were the first to take advantage of innovations ranging from movable type to the telephone.

4. *There is an uneven distribution of ability to make use of new communication techniques and technologies.* A certain degree of ability to use new technology can probably be called "innate," but it is important to note that much *acquired* knowledge and skill is directly related to the ability to acquire more information. In some cases the key

200

is technical knowledge (for example, how to use a computer or string a radio antenna). In other cases, higher degrees of literacy are necessary to enable people to make larger gains when given access to new technology. (What good is computerized access to all the published works of man if the potential user cannot understand the language of most of the authors?) In still other cases, training is required for the efficient use of even simple techniques. (The old telegraph key, the library catalogue, postal zip codes and UHF channel tuning are examples.)

5. *There seems to be a correlation between initial information level and the motivation to use new communication techniques.* The roots of this phenomenon are complex and poorly understood. Those with higher initial information levels seem more inclined to *seek* additional information. This aspect of the relationship between initial levels and information gain may result from social pressure, differential perceived rewards, or other social psychological phenomena. It appears consistently over a wide range of situations.

Proposition 4: Humans have a limited capacity to process and store information.

One person may be able to take in more than another person per unit time, and there are undoubtedly great differences in memory. Mnemonic techniques and training can increase human channel capacity and storage capability. Yet it seems reasonable to suppose that there are limits to the amount of information any individual can successfully digest or retain. (11)

Such analysis, of course, speaks only to the troublesome

201

question of the *quantity* of information received by individuals. However, it leads to conclusions that may seem to mitigate some of the more disturbing of the "widening–gap" effects. If information–rich individuals achieve full use of a new communication technology, they cannot further improve their use of that technology. Relatively information–poor groups will then *close the gap over the long run,* since they tend to move toward the asymptote–although at a slower rate. For example, literacy among Italian brides and grooms showed this effect. (4, pp. 122–23) The criterion was ability to sign one's name, and the gap between men and women grew larger until 1880. From then on, however, women steadily closed the literacy gap. (See Figure 1.) The pattern is one of a widening initial gap followed by a catch–up period for the relatively disadvantaged. [8]

If *human* information processing ability were the key limiting factor upon the impact of communication technology, then technological change would eventually lead to a situation in which all people were brought to their maximum potential through technology. The information–rich could not go beyond their full potential, and the information–poor would close the gap over the long run. Differences between individuals and groups would be the result of innate, rather than environmental factors. Unfortunately, this utopian vision of each person having the opportunity to make full use of his or her potential capacity is shattered by the implications of the next two propositions.

Proposition 5: Compared with humans, machines now have virtually unlimited capacity to process and store information.

Training and access to computers, satellites, and other technologies give the information—rich a different type of advantage over the information—poor. It is not just a case of their having seen, read, or heard more than other people. The advantaged group has a staggering amount of *potential* information available that others cannot begin to tap. (The argument is one that has been used by successful encyclopedia salesmen for years. If you do not have access to information, contained in twenty volumes plus a yearbook, you and your family will fall behind those who do.)

In an urban technological society, the difference between those with and those without access to new communication and information—handling devices often produces a difference between a group that controls its own affairs and a group that is totally dependent on the paternalistic benevolence of the information handlers. In the past, an illiterate could always go off to fend (however abjectly) for himself. He could talk to people and accumulate information from verbal sources. The modern "illiterate" is to a greater extent at the mercy of his sources of information. Machines compute his tax bill (or welfare check) from information he often does not have and does not understand. Policy decisions about amortization of A. T. & T. long lines, legal requirements for UHF tuning, or radio or television frequency allocations influence his environment although he may not be aware that there has been an issue—let alone a decision.

The limits of naked human ability have become irrelevant. It is as though we had been considering how fast man could move across the face of the earth but had limited our discussions to the types of shoes that might help a runner break the four—minute mile. For all practical purposes, the discussion of limited human abilities can almost completely ignore memory, although the limits of the human ability to process amounts of information per unit time still remain. (You have to read the computer output or watch the TV program.) And new techniques give machines the burden of selecting appropriate material for an individual's use, so the quality of material received per unit of time is improved. Unequal access to new technology bypasses the gap—closing effects of human limitations.

In a theoretical closed system, this would still not matter much because we would expect the long—run gap—closing effects of saturation as everyone gradually became able to use the new technologies. But the world is not a closed system.[9] New technologies are replaced by newer technologies.

Proposition 6: New communication techniques and technologies create new information gaps before old gaps close.

The fact that approximately the same proportion of wives and husbands can now sign their names speaks to the closing of a gap on an outdated criterion. By the time the literacy gap between men and women closed, a better criterion of communication skills might have been a high school education; and by the time that gap closed, the criterion might have become a college education. Women are still behind men because the empirical criteria for success changed before they closed the gap on the older criteria.

We can generalize this phenomenon to all groups with different initial information levels. *The gap—widening effect is usually sustained by a given technique until a new technique is introduced—and the information gap is further widened.* The children of the information—rich use techniques their parents never dreamed of, while the children of the information—poor fall farther behind (although they are above the levels attained by the earlier generations in their own group).

Techniques that make possible mass production of cheap paperback books undoubtedly raise the number of books read by low readership groups. The same techniques also widen the gap between high and low readership. In the long run, there is a finite limit to the number of books an individual can read, so the gap in book reading might close. By that time, however, the number of books read would probably be a meaningless criterion, and social impact might be related to different communication techniques plus access to potential information. In that case, the high readership group would undoubtedly be the first to use the new techniques.

Figure 1 presents one way to look at the effects of these six propositions. It combines a hypothetical description with some juxtaposed data that fit the ideal pattern. The proportion of an operationally defined information—rich group (husbands) that meets a criterion measure of information (ability to sign name) increases more rapidly than the proportion among a corresponding information—poor group (brides). G_2 is larger than G_1. Although the latter group begins to close the gap (G_4 is smaller than G_3, which is

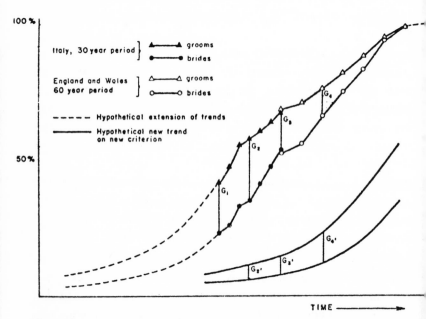

Figure 1: Proportions of different subgroups meeting a criterion over time

smaller than G_2), a new criterion measure (e.g., six years of schooling) is introduced, and a new gap (G_2 to G_3 to G_4) begins to widen.

To review some different supporting evidence, consider the university as a technique for transmitting information. Jencks and Riesman (6, p. 95) report that between 1915 and 1925 the rate of college entrance among male high school graduates "ranged from 43 percent among those whose fathers had not finished elementary school to 64 percent among those whose fathers had entered college." The comparable figures during the 1945–1955 period were 31 percent and 84 percent. Jencks and Riesman add that "(if) we look at a college freshman's chances of completing four years, we find a similar widening of the gap between the advantaged and the disadvantaged."

The widening gap tends to be associated with initial economic and/or informational status more clearly than it is associated with personal ability.

Although data presented by Jencks and Riesman (6, p. 103) indicate a strong relationship between aptitude (on a standard test) and entry into college, there is a strong relationship between *status* and college entry within each aptitude level.

The TV program *Sesame Street* is a new communication technique that explicitly attempts to *narrow* the information gap by providing preliminary training in basic skills to pre–school children. The innovation in this case was a new type of television *content.* After the first year of operation,

207

the data in Table 1 were issued by Ball and Bogatz in *The First Year of Sesame Street: An Evaluation.* (2)[10]

The maximum score was 203; data represent 943 total children—731 disadvantaged, 169 advantaged, and 43 Spanish speaking not separately presented in Table 1. Even without the raw data and the appropriate statistical tests, we can make several suppositions on the basis of these figures:

1. There is a relationship between use of the program and ability measured *before* the children had seen the program. The more a child needed the information in *Sesame Street,* the less frequently he or she would watch it.

2. Without controlling for amount of viewing, we find more gain for groups with higher initial scores. The gap widens. (The effect of the program may not be to widen the gap when amount of viewing and home background are con-

Table 1: Pretest and gain scores on battery of achievement tests by amount of Sesame Street viewing and background

	Quartile (Q_1 viewed least, Q_4 most)			
	Q_1	Q_2	Q_3	Q_4
Background				
Total				
pretest	76	86	94	101
gain	19	31	39	48
Disadvantaged				
pretest	76	84	87	97
gain	19	29	37	47
Advantaged				
pretest	95	102	113	110
gain	27	38	40	45

208

trolled. The appropriate data are not available.

3. In the first three viewing quartiles, there was more gain for advantaged children (who had higher initial scores) than for disadvantaged children. With viewing held constant in this crude way, we still find a widening gap. The advantaged children scored higher to begin with and made greater gains within each of the first three viewing quartiles. (Home environment is not controlled, but this is the way communication techniques have social impact. They do not appear in the world as single independent variables in a controlled experiment.)

4. Only in the highest quartile (which included children said to have viewed *Sesame Street* more than five times a week) does the gap fail to widen. The hopeful sign here is that when the fullest use is made of a new technique, the the gap—widening influences may be avoided.[11]

Lest we suppose that the widening gap as a result of educational and cultural uses of television is confined to children, we should consider Bower's results (3, pp. 51–53) from a major national survey of television viewing habits. He reported that only 27 percent of the population with a grade—school education were able to receive signals from a public television station, while 63 percent of the college—educated could receive these stations. In addition, when he examined only those people who could receive public TV signals in their homes, he found that 24 percent of the grade—school—educated, 35 percent of the high—school—educated, and 49 percent of the college—educated watched such stations at least once a week. If we are willing to make certain assumptions about the meaning of college

209

education and the content of public television, it becomes clear that the growth of public television has had a gap—widening effect.

When communication techniques are applied to social problems, the political implications of the widening gap between information—rich and poor become critical.

Public policy, if it wishes to narrow (or avoid widening) the gap, must move toward a planned program for the actual use of communication techniques by the information—poor. Short of putting the information—rich group in detention centers where they are denied access to media, there is probably no easy way to circumvent the widening gap. Improvements in information—processing techniques have the greatest impact on those who are in the best position to use them.

A more realistic approach to communication policy in regard to the information gap confronts the issue in a different way. Instead of asking how to keep the gap from getting wider, public policy can direct itself to the question of which background factors determine the initial levels upon which there are differential effects. If the information—rich and the information—poor are primarily economic or geographic or racial castes—and not differentiated by ability across economic, geographic or racial barriers—then the ideal of advancement based on merit is not attained. In such cases a widening gap is maintained by barriers that are contrary to the philosophy espoused by our society. Programs for moving

210

toward the ideal must stem from public policy designed not to narrow the information gap, but to guarantee that the factors producing the gap are related to ability.

One approach has been the simple expedient of providing equal access to new techniques. *Sesame Street* is available free of charge to all groups in all parts of the country. Assuming equal availability of TV sets (a fair assumption) and equal ability to receive public TV stations (an unfair assumption, as Bower's data show), the program and its information are distributed across economic, geographic, and racial barriers. The liberal assumption is that when the economic barriers to media use are eliminated, any gap will be the product of differential ability.

Such approaches are expedients. They meet the political requirements without actually changing much. (The children of the information—rich watch *Sesame Street* more, even though it is available to all.) So—called "radical" approaches to media use recognize this. But the radicals too often demand compensatory funds to produce self—serving and marginally used content that does little to redistribute media *use*. The problem is that economically and socially deprived individuals are also handicapped by motivational factors and other aspects of their psychological environments. Someone with the ability to make full use of communication technology may not want to bother with it when his environment is not supportive. Someone with marginal ability may be spurred to use new techniques by a supportive environment. Free public schools and libraries have been available longer than *Sesame Street*, and the pattern of their utilization has widened the information gap. The answer is not only to produce programs

211

"for the poor" if the poor are not watching. The question is not just "How can we provide equal access?" but also "How can we insure equal use?"

Simple solutions to motivational and environmental problems underlying unequal use of media do not seem likely. How can the poor make better use of the telephones, radios, and televisions they have? Equal access is a necessary but not sufficient condition for equal use. (And the political obstacles to some types of equal access should not be minimized.) But the goal of an information gap that is solely the product of differential ability cannot be reached until individuals in all social strata have an equal desire to *use* communication techniques.

REFERENCES

1.   Bagdikian, Ben H. *The Information Machines*. New York: Harper & Row, 1971.

2.   Ball, S., and G. A. Bogatz, *The First Year of Sesame Street: An Evaluation*. Princeton, N.J.: Educational Testing Service, 1970.

3.   Bower, R. T. *Television and the Public*. New York: Holt, Rhinehart and Winston, 1973.

4.   Cipolla, C. M. *Literacy and Development in the West*. Baltimore, Md.: Penguin Books, 1969.

5.   Ellul, Jacques. *The Technological Society*. New York: Vintage Books, 1964.

6.   Jencks, Christopher, and David Riesman. *The Academic Revolution*. New York: Doubleday, 1968.

212

7. Katzman, Natan. " Communication Flow and Social Entropy." *Ekistics* 172, 1970, pp. 212–219.

8. Katzman, Natan. "Social Entropy and Communication Systems." Paper presented to the annual meeting of the International Communication Association, Minneapolis, Minnesota, 1970.

9. Meier, R. L. *A Communications Theory of Urban Growth.* Boston: M.I.T. Press, 1962.

10. Mesthene, E. G. *Technological Change.* New York: Mentor, 1970.

11. Miller, G. A. "The Magical Number Seven, Plus or Minus Two." *Psychological Review 63*, 1956, pp. 81–97.

12. Rogers, E. M. *Communication of Innovations.* New York: The Free Press, 1971.

---

[1]The term *technology* has been used to cover broad concepts encompassing diverse phenomena. It might be appealing to use "technique" as Ellul (5) used the term; however, the connotations of "communication technique" seem to imply a misleading emphasis on interpersonal behavior. Mesthene's (10, p. 25) definition of "technology as the organization of knowledge for the achievement of practical purposes," provides a useful conceptualization that includes both mechanical and intellectual tools. Since it is not the purpose of this paper to coin neologisms or attempt to use terms that may have misleading connotations,

the issue will be evaded through loose reference to both technique and technology.

[2] The ideas presented here are not entirely new or original. Some have been discussed as peripheral issues by scholars concerned with things such as the impact of the stirrup on feudal Europe, the process of adopting Modern Math in elementary schools, and the effects of cable television systems. I am indebted to many friends and colleagues for their ideas, insights, and criticisms.

[3] One problem with a discussion of these issues is the lack of a clear meaning for the term "information." There are two competing definitions. One involves the idea of patterned matter and/or energy. The other involves the idea of a change of state. The former is *source oriented*: to transmit information is to impose pattern on matter or energy (by writing or by broadcasting radio waves, for example). The latter is *receiver oriented*: to receive information is to be changed (by knowing something unknown before the information arrived). Both definitions have merit when communication technology is considered. The mass media—those which distribute a single message to many people— are most easily studied at the source of communication. Systems designed to provide information from many sources to a single individual (such as libraries or information—retrieval systems) are most easily studied from the viewpoint of the receiver. Technologies that are related to interpersonal communication (telephones and postal systems, for example) tend to require a combination of the two points of view.

[4] It may seem that this premise verges on being part of a circular relationship: that which improves communication is

technology, and technology improves communication. However, technique and technology are not necessarily improvements. Nor must they increase overall information levels.
Within the meaning of technological change is the possibility
of change to lower quantities and qualities of communication.
Thus, we hear the argument that the introduction of television lowered the "quality" of culture and information from
levels attained in the print era. There is always the
possibility that a new technique will kill off an old one and
create a net loss in transmitted information. I do not wish to
propose that this has ever happened; but the premise, although not profound, is not true by definition. The key is
that *communication technologies allow communication to
take place*. They need not transmit information any better
than earlier techniques, but they will grow and survive only
if they are better, cheaper, or have some other *relative
advantage* over older techniques.

[5] The *hubit* is a term introduced by Meier (9, p. 131):
"A *hubit* is a bit of meaningful *information* received by a
single human being. The same bit may have been received by
other persons...According to classical information theory the
receipt of this knowledge by an extra individual is redundant...(Thus) per capita flows needed a new designation, and
hubits seemed to have appropriate connotations." Perhaps
the designation *man—bits* would have helped. If six men
each receive the same five *bits* of information, 30 *hubits*
will be accumulated. The six men received five *hubits per
capita*, rather than the 1.25 *bits per capita* that standard
information theory would report.

[6] The *dichotomy* between the so—called "rich" and

215

"poor" individuals in society may sometimes prove mis-leading. It is probably better to think in terms of bi-modal or multi-modal *continua* of initial information levels.

[7] Deliberate government policy sometimes gives poor schools a first chance to use a new technology. However, such pilot projects do not negate the general trend in a free-market school system. The exception does point to possible political decisions to dampen the gap-widening tendency.

[8] The problem of *ceilings* sometimes confounds empirical studies of the gap between subgroups. In many cases it is logically impossible for a variable to go above a given value--e.g., 100 percent of the subgroup meet a criterion, or the mean score on a test is a perfect score. In such cases gaps cannot widen. When one group approaches a natural asymptote, operational definitions (i.e., criteria) must usually be changed if there is to be fruitful consideration of gaps. (See Proposition 6).

[9] A thermodynamic model of the relationship between communication to and from a social system and the changing structure of that system is presented in two earlier papers (7, 8). The present discussion focuses on a narrow aspect of that generalization. *New technology facilitates inter-systemic communication and raises intra-systemic negen-tropy.*

[10] It should be noted that these data are taken from various sections of the report. Ball and Bogatz do not deal with the types of comparisons made here. They do demonstrate the relationship between viewing and gain; but since the test is is a test of material presented in the program, the finding is not very exciting.

216

[11] Many of the children in the highest quartile undoubtedly were in enriched experimental conditions created by the research project. Some children were encouraged to view at home, and some children were exposed to the program in preschool settings. (How else could 25 percent of all children studied be found to view the program more than five times a week?) Again, lack of data makes interpretation speculative. However, we may suppose that these techniques saturated the children with *Sesame Street* and managed to wipe out the differences in home background. Note that the Q_4 disadvantaged group actually pulled ahead of the Q_1 and Q_2 advantaged groups (final score equals pretest plus gain). This is somewhat mitigated by the fact that the disadvantaged Q_4 group had a mean pretest score roughly the same as the mean pretest scores for the advantaged Q_1 and Q_2 groups. Thus, it is hard to conclude that the ''background'' (and/or ability) of the former was worse than that of the latter; and consequent higher gains may be attributable to higher viewing levels for initially similar children.

13

THE ILLUSIONS OF CABLE TELEVISION

Monroe E. Price

*Cable television, it is said, will have
dramatic consequences for the quality of life
in the cities, for the delivery of health and
educational services, for the way people get
their news, buy and pay for goods, learn about
candidates and vote for them. Really?*

Cable is emerging at a time when mature technologies are everywhere being questioned. But, curiously, doubts about technology have been turned to the advantage of cable. There is a deep—seated feeling that if previous system—perturbating "advances" had been well thought out, we would not be in such deep trouble today: if only we had been more thoughtful about the automobile, or at least the development of the highway system; if only in the 1940's we had been more sagacious and deliberate about the way television had entered our lives; if only we had looked adequately into the future when patterns and styles

218

of housing development were fostered by the federal government in the 1940's. Cable is offered as a cure. The answer to the problems of old machines is a new machine.

Cable, together with satellite capability for long–distance transmission and less expensive production expenses, is seen as the base of a system which can pinpoint differentiated audiences and make it economical to serve them. Broadcast economics will be replaced by cable economics; the need to serve mass audiences will be supplemented by the viability of serving smaller, more intensive ones. By revoutionizing the way information is generated and distributed, by decentralizing and dehomogenizing the content, some hope to reverse strong trends in American society. The hope is for program content on cable which is sharply differentiated along lines of language, race, employment, culture, geography, and interest.

Others, including Peter Goldmark, the former sage of CBS and now an independent seer, look to cable as a technique for repopulating areas of the United States which have been drained as part of the movement toward urbanization. In a sense, they argue, the attraction of the city, both in a commercial and an entertainment sense, flows from the concentration of information and communications capacity there. By immersing rural areas in communications capacity, the Goldmark school seeks to reverse the trend toward population concentration.

As if these expectations were not a sufficient burden. cable is also perceived as a machine for an increase in participatory democracy. Under the present scheme, it is alleged, the vast power of the television medium is closely held by the networks (and, some would add, by the U.S.

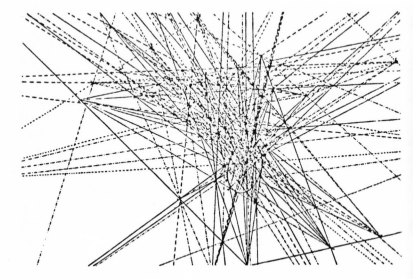

government). Even the power of station licensees is not a sufficient counterweight.

A kind of crisis in the administration of broadcasting's fairness doctrine has resulted from the gap between the lack of equality of access in fact and a general commitment to equality of opportunity for competing points of view to reach the public at large.

In this crisis over access which has afflicted the broadcast television system, cable television emerges again as a kind of knight on a white horse. Problems of access, it is said, are merely a function of scarce resources. It is only because there are so few channels that we are tremendously worried about fairness. Where there are only one or two channels in a community, there is a public duty

220

to make sure that it does not fall into the hands of one viewpoint.

Cable, it is said, eliminates scarcity, eliminates the monopoly status of the programmer, and therefore eliminates the chaos and anxiety that surround implementation of the fairness doctrine. With many channels, competing views can find an opportunity to reach an audience, constrained only by a more or less market—established price mechanism. Problems of the very poor obtaining access would remain, but other objectionable features of the present system of controlled access would be modified.

Other promises have come out of the dream machine of cable television. It is supposed to provide riches to the almost bankrupt cities, bring ballet nightly to the ballet—omane, challenge the power and influence of A.T.&T., disalienate the youth, and provide hope and comfort for the elderly.

Is it all illusion? Is there a bandwagon
psychology to cable which has
drawn a great variety of interests?

The frank answer, after five years of research in the United States, is that we do not know. Much of the existing research, the product of foundation grants, is largely anec—dotal. One essay collects information on existing law enforcement applications of cable systems; another looks at how cable systems have been employed for health serv—ices. But there are too few examples; when the systems studied are small and atypical, it is difficult to provide an

221

adequate idea of scope and cost, of the possibility of replication. More useful have been research efforts, usually by economists, that try to assess the impact of cable growth on the health of broadcasting stations and the great television networks. These studies have been productive, but they do not tell us much about what a basically cable system will mean for the distribution of information in the United States.

A third category of research includes the inventive essays wherein the authors attempt to provide a sense of the future without too heavy an anchoring in the past. These are the most illusionistic efforts as well as the most imaginative. They are the most needed, but the least reliable. Worse, the enthusiasm of the researcher is often a reflection of the market for foundation—supported research. Pictures of the brave new world which resemble the existing one do not sell. So a premium is placed on revolutionary ways to get the news, shop, do business, relate to others.

It is hard to pinpoint how much exactly has been spent on cable—related communications research in the United States, but government and foundation support probably exceeds $5 million. The initial government—sponsored research was through the President's Task Force on Communications Policy in 1970. In the summer of 1970, the Sloan Foundation announced a major grant, approximately $500,000, to establish the Sloan Commission on Cable Communications, to provide guidance on the future potential of cable, particularly in the cities. The Commission itself became a granting agency seeking guidance from a large

222

number of persons about the possible impact of cable on society.

Given these considerable expenditures, why is it that we are not closer to the answer to the basic question—namely, whether or not cable is an illusion? Why are we so prone to accept the dream? Agencies and interests savor the potential of the solutions and often do not wish to be hindered or obstructed by the lack of facts. In their competition for budget increases, innovation or purported innovation may be rewarded; as long as cable has the ring of the new about it, funds are forthcoming.

Another implied threat is used to justify accelerated action by government and foundations even when the groundwork is unfinished. Cable is like the ring at the merry−go−round, it is said. If it isn't grabbed off now by the public, it will be grabbed off by someone else. Cable will grow; it will spread throughout the cities. The question is not whether it will expand, but how.

Educators now assume that cable will come and that it will, on balance, be a benefit. The chore is to justify the greatest dedication of cable assets to the educational mission. Advocates of public access take much the same view, urging the reservation of channels for public use on a common−carrier basis in each major cable system. Basic questions go by the boards; they have not been asked and they may never be asked.

But some rumination on the fundamental questions ought to be indulged. If they were answered, we might

gain some insight into the question of whether
cable is an illusion or not.

For example, how can we speak intelligently about kinds of distribution systems for information until we are in a better position to evaluate the utility of competing forms of communication? In the rush to make available adequate facilities for the simultaneous distribution of numerous television signals, we know precious little about the value of television over radio, of color over black and white, of television and radio over print, and of increased human relationships over all of them.

Just as basic, and just as unknown, is the question of the relationship between the viewer and the television set. Cable is a distribution mechanism, and, at present, that is all. Sometime in the future, cable will provide the opportunity for the viewer to interact with the message through a primitive but increasingly complex response device. But at present, the utility of cable is based on the increased potential and choice in the number of television signals which can be distributed to each receiving set. We cannot assign a value to the new abundance until we know the value of the individual signal.

An example is in the field of education. Cable television can certainly augment the capacity of a school to use television as part of its teaching mission. There is enhanced flexibility in scheduling and less competition for time. But the fundamental knowledge about how television itself is useful in education is a prerequisite for knowing how valuable more television can be. It is true that a different

224

system (with more economical use of central facilities, greater utility in instructing teachers, a great possibility of restructuring the curriculum around the new technology) implies far more of an improvement than would be suggested by multiplying the number of old channels to obtain the number of new channels; but still there is the basic question of the relationship between the students and the set, how it affects them.

Another example comes from health services. When the Sloan Commission first began to explore this subject, it gathered together a number of health experts, some of whom had had familiarity with public information and the use of television. Their question, their basic skepticism, related not to cable, but to the capacity of the health professions to use any vehicle of public information wisely for all but the most limited purposes. For the question was not how many channels were available, but do we really know what to say? Do we know how we want the viewer to react? Do we know what we want him to do? Can we advise him to do anything but see a doctor? And can we do that in light of the shortage of medical resources?

In this class of issues there is also an aesthetic one. What is the relationship between television content, habitual watching of television, and one's view of the world? In a nibbling way, that question is now being asked in America with respect to violence on television and with respect to children's television in general. It is always asked by advertisers who are making economic decisions about the use of television. We have a vague sense that television has affected our culture, but we do not know how.

Is greater insight into this basic question a precondition to intelligent planning for cable? It may be that making television more appealing, resulting in a greater number of hours devoted to television viewing, does not serve the public interest. To what extent do we wish to become more dependent upon the electrical transmission of images? The question is not only difficult to answer, it is hard to articulate.

There is also a set of more tangible basic questions about the illusion of cable's promise. The adequate use of cable television for non—entertainment purposes means great changes in the bureaucracies which run those services. In discussing education, for example, it is facile to talk of the dedication of one or seven or ten channels to schools. But that is only the beginning of the inquiry. There is no ground to believe that schools, increasingly unionized, rigid in structure, would (or ought to) reshuffle themselves so as to incorporate the potential of cable television in a complete and generous way. Much the same doubt can be expressed about the capacity or willingness of other substantial bureaucracies to change to accommodate the potential of television.

Related is the difficult question of assessing whether scarce education (or other service) dollars should be expended to adjust to cable or to incorporate other innovations. It has generally been true that persons writing in the field of technological innovation in service delivery have quickly become partisans of the particular technological innovation which they are studying and have not evaluated the benefits of alternative innovations.

226

Besides, the difficult budgetary decisions concerning the introduction of cable are often masked under the assumption that the capital cost of the system will be borne by the home subscriber (who will pay for most of the basic system so that his entertainment choices are heightened) and that service users can pay marginal rather than average costs for channel use. It is unclear that this common basis for computing charges should or will continue. But a shift in the financing burden from entertainment users of cable to non-entertainment users would mean that the comparative value of the technology would be lessened.

We are left, then, with a cable technology which, all agree, will grow with medium speed during the next decade. It is almost certain that the innovation will mean a richer choice in entertainment offerings on television for millions of Americans. What is in greater doubt is the likelihood that cable will be a contributor to the solution of public problems.

PART IV. CAPABILITIES FOR SPECIALIZED REPORTING

Previously in this book we have seen that existing media are becoming more specialized and that new media will create still more opportunities for specialized communication. But we have also concluded that the institutions which control these media hold the key to their future. One of the most important of these instututions is the profession of journalism, and it is to the capabilities of this profession that we turn in this final section of the book.

Many would argue that in a period of societal fragmentation and specialization in communication that the media should attempt to maintain a mass audience so that they can bridge the gap between the specialized communities of interest. Others would argue that that kind of communication never has existed and that the general interest publication should be forsaken. A part of the actual situation probably exists in each of these positions. Audiences of a given medium probably always have been relatively homogeneous. For example, research on science communication has documented that consumers of science news in news

228

papers or on television generally are more educated and have more background in science than does the average news consumer. Yet these consumers still have less specialized interests that do the readers of *Scientific American, Science*, or of technical journals.

In other words, there are degrees of specialized interests in audiences, including the highly involved specialist or member of an interest group, the interested layman or non-member, and the uninterested non-reader. Highly specialized media do and will cater to the specialist; general interest media will appeal to a conglomeration of interests. Neither will or could attract someone who is uninterested or uninvolved in a particular subject.

Many of the highly specialized media are staffed by professionally trained journalists, although most journalists work for the "mass" media. Mass media could be accurately described as semi—specialized media which provide information to a number of semi—involved communities of interest. Seldom do individuals attend to all of the information in the medium, only to that which pertains to their community of interest. Thus, in an era when most media will be specialized to some degree, the journalist will have to be a mediator with a foot in two camps——that of the specialist and that of the interested layman. His role will be to filter and translate highly technical information that the layman can apply to his life situation or which will help the layman understand the complex environment in which he lives. Likewise, the journalist will have to interpret the specialized interests of involved groups such as blacks, women, young people, and local communities to those who are not involved but still interested in that group.

By and large, the chapters in Part IV show that journalism still has a distance to travel to meet this goal, but in each case the authors point out the necessity for specialized reporting and offer suggestions for its improvement. In the first chapter, Meyer describes how a reporter can apply social science techniques to reporting in order to do a more specialized and accurate job of reporting politics and other social phenomena. Cohn and Friedman then examine changes in science writing over the past 20 years. Today, they conclude, fewer reporters move from general assignment reporting to the science beat as they have done in the past. Instead, they are coming into journalism with special training in the sciences. Friedman also reports that science writers now more often attempt to relate science to the lives of readers and less often attempt to use science to arouse the reader's curiosity. Cohn gives examples of this relevance in reporting by describing his experiences writing about doctors, hospitals, and health services––the point at which "science and the layman truly meet."

Ward describes the types of people and techniques he has observed as a broadcast reporter covering research on and speculations about the future. Although he concludes that specialist reporters have always existed and that more will be needed, he adds that there will always be a need for the generalist.

Finally, Pollock, and Grunig explore areas of specialized reporting where the media have been and still are deficient. Few reporters have specialized knowledge of consumer problems or of social science. Research by Rubin and Sachs shows the same to be true for environmental problems.[1] Most reporters have been shifted to these beats from general beats, much as science reporters were shifted 10 to 20 years ago. Likewise, environmental and consumer reporters are hampered in their efforts because it is difficult to report information that might do harm to the interests of advertisers which support the medium. These final chapters also show that, in general, specialized reporting is limited to those major metropolitan newspapers which have more educated and sophisticated audiences.

[1]David M. Rubin and David P. Sachs, *Mass Media and the Environment* (New York: Praeger Special Studies, 1973), pp. 36–53.

14

THE FUTURE OF SOCIAL SCIENCE TECHNIQUES IN REPORTING

Philip Meyer

Most of my modest success in popularizing the use of social science methods in reporting is due to the fact that Everette Dennis, who chronicles new developments in journalism, told me what to call this thing that I do.[1] It's difficult being an innovator if there is no label for the innovation. I had thought I was just an ordinary reporter until I gave a lecture at Kansa State University where Prof. Dennis told me my kind of reporting was "precision journalism." Before meeting Dennis, I was working on a book to be called, "The Application of Social and Behavioral Science Research Methods to the Practice of Journalism". I promptly changed the title to *Precision Journalism*.[2]

I learned that precision journalism––without the label–– was possible when I covered my first big story. I was in the city room of the Topeka *Daily Capital* in 1951 covering a flood. The weather bureau called it a hundred–year flood, the kind that pours so much rain in the river valley that the water rises to a height you can expect to see only once every hundred years or so. The flood covered quite a bit of downtown Topeka and other cities in the Kansas River basin and became an immediate political issue. The Army Corps of Engineers and the downstream interests in Kansas City had been lobbying Congress for a large appropriation for a series of dams in the valley.

The chief of the corps of engineers said that if three previously proposed dams had been built, this flood would not have occurred. Therefore he proposed that Congress should now appropriate the money to prevent another flood.

That seemed logical, but James L. Robinson the state editor——my boss——on the *Daily Capital* got out a pad and pencil and did some calculations. He learned from the weather bureau that the average flow during the flood was 215,000 cubic feet per second over a period of 147 hours. With these statistics, he figured exactly how many acre feet of storage space behind the reservoirs would be needed to contain the flood. Then he checked the number of acre feet that had been designed into those dams that the corps of engineers had wanted to build and found that even if all the flood waters had fallen behind the dams——which they wouldn't have done——that the dikes still would have been topped. That flood was such a unique and unusual occurrence that none of the plans on the books would have worked.

The resulting story was a fairly major expose done by an editor with a pad and a pencil who knew how to add, subtract, multiply and divide——which is of course, a fairly unusual skill among newspaper persons.

Shortly after, the corps of engineers revised its plan, calling for seven dams instead of three. Kansas is now a fine state for boating and swimming, and I hope I live long

233

enough to see the next hundred—year flood so that I can find out whether the dams really work or not.

Reporters have always been more competent if they have been able to count. In the future, more reporters will need that capability. That does not mean they have to be full—fledged social scientists. Many reporters are capable of "precision journalism" and don't realize it. Believe it or not, a reporter can make his stories more readable when he puts numbers in them. If you think about it, you will realize that we have something of a national passion for numbers.

We like things that can be counted, measured, divided. We like football games, for example, because we can measure progress in yards on the field or in seconds on the clock. Most government policies that require innovation are justified through quantitative methods. If you want to achieve a humanistic goal, for example, changing a government policy to make the world better, you should be prepared to use counting and measuring devices to demonstrate that the world will be better or else it will be difficult to support your case.

Some people say that intangible things are more important simply because they are intangible. We are humanists, they say, not quantifiers. But that's not so. Take for example, the trouble people go to just to count money. Economists can do very imaginative things with data because good records are kept about where money goes and who does what with it. Anything that involves being born and dying also can be easily quantified. The events are unambiguous, and the record keeping is reliable.

Most of the main social indicators, numbers that are watched to see if the world is getting better or worse, involve things like counting money, births and deaths.

234

Lately social scientists have started to count things that aren't so easy to interpret. For example, good records are kept on divorces. Thus, we know that divorce rates have gone up fairly spectacularly in recent years. Now is this a good sign or a bad sign? One interpretation might be that unhappy marriages are easier to end then they used to be. Another might be that people are getting so mean and nasty that many men and women can no longer live together for any length of time.

To find out which explanation is more plausible, you have to go and ask people. You have to look for variables that are really inside their heads. These are soft indicators, something you cannot get simply from analyzing public records. Many social scientists are pushing this soft indicator business as far as they can, and their main tool is survey research. One of my favorite people in this business is Angus Campbell at the University of Michigan. Campbell is concentrating on a limited number of these possible indicators. One of them is the degree to which the government irritates people.

The election surveys of the University of Michigan Survey Research Center show that public confidence in government is going downhill steeply. The decline started in the early 1960's about the time of the Kennedy assassination. The Vietnam War might have had something to do with it. But no one is really quite sure what has caused the decline. Public confidence started to level off in early 1972, but after Watergate it dropped to fantastic lows.

One of the basic questions which the survey asks is:

"Do you think government in Washington can be trusted all of the time, most of the time or only some of the time?" When that question was first asked in the 1950's, the researchers had no category for "none of the time." Now that's how many people respond. At the same time people now have more numerous and more complicated interactions with government because government performs many more services than ever before. Few of us can pass through any significant period of our lives without encountering somebody in the bureaucracy. So trust in government becomes more and more important if government is to keep operating. That's why Campbell is working on his "index of official insolence." He takes the name from a phrase in Hamlet's soliloquoy. "Who would bear the whips and scorns of time, the oppressor's wrong, the proud man's contumely, the pangs of despised love, the law's delay, the insolence of office." That's a nice list of social indicators.

The University of Michigan researchers found another interesting statistic in a special indicator project. In 1955, 21 percent of the husbands in Detroit got their own breakfast as opposed to 32 percent in 1971.

Obviously the world is changing, and we in journalism are in a position to watch some of those changes coming over the horizon. Precision journalists are reporters sitting on a watchtower and watching the horizon. Sometimes we don't recognize what we saw coming until it's already here and it's too late to do anything about it. The current wave of nostalgia provides a good example. Many people now are finding value in things that existed in the recent past. My daughter went to a high school dance which had the theme

236

of behaving like teenagers did in the 1950's. They got a few things mixed up. They swallowed the goldfish, and we never did that in the 1950's. But they did wear bobby socks. Teenagers see the film "American Grafitti" and wish they had been teenagers when it looked like teenagers had more fun.

A survey published in 1971 could have predicted the nostalgia wave.[3] The survey provided the first sign that people were thinking of the past as better than the future—— a very abnormal thing, in our society at least. The survey used a social science device called a self–anchoring scale. The respondent is asked to imagine the best possible future for himself or the best possible future for his country and the worst possible future for himself and his country. Then he's shown a picture of a ladder with steps numbered from one to ten and asked, "On which step of the ladder do you think the United States is at the present time?"

The respondent usually puts the nation a step or so above the middle. Next he's asked where he thinks the United States stood on this ladder five years ago, then, where it will be five years in the future.

Normally, most respondents indicate a lower rung on the ladder for five years ago and a higher position for the future.

That question had been asked for a number of years in a number of different countries making possible a cross national comparison of the upward pattern that was almost always displayed until 1971. Ominously, in that year, the average position on the ladder for the present was lower than for the past. Americans were saying the nation had peaked, that we were a better country five years ago. While

237

they expected some improvement in the future, you could see this sense of national gloom two years before Watergate. There were many reasons for people to be gloomy but nobody realized the national mood was changing until the survey revealed the trend.

Journalists who know how to count and measure things can spot such trends. They can also check on government officials who use statistics to cover their errors. A North—western University psychologist, Donald Campbell, has made a list of statistical fallacies that "trapped adminis—trators," use when their projects turn sour. Journalists fall for them frequently. When I was covering education in Miami, the school board found that it could save money by televising lectures on closed circuit television. The best teachers would lecture throughout the school system by television while the less qualified teachers would supervise the students as they watched television in the classroom.

Students took tests before and after they were exposed to the television courses and were compared to a control group of students who did not use television. Sure enough, the television kids did better, and that was that.

I have always wanted to go back to Miami and find out what happened to the television classes three or four years later. A classic effect in educational experiments is called the Hawthorne effect, and it says that people who are experimental subjects may perform better simply because they know they are in an experiment and believe something more is expected of them.

In some industrial experiments you never worry about Hawthorne effect because as long as the workers produce

238

more, it makes little difference whether the reason is the Hawthorne effect or the color of the walls. The increased production is real. But in educational experiments the optimistic press releases soon stop and few reporters think to go back and look two or three years later when the innovation may have been forgotten because it was found to have no lasting value after all.

Administrators also use a device called regression toward the mean which can help make a reform look successful. Reforms are usually initiated when the thing being reformed is at its worst. The classic example is a program to cut down on drunk driving in Connecticut in the 1950's. The number of deaths from automobile accidents went down 12 per cent afterwards, and the governor said the program had definitely been successful because it cut traffic deaths by 12 per cent. But if you look at the traffic deaths in Connecticut over a long period of time you see that a variation of 12 per cent or more is not particularly unusual. The reforms had been initiated immediately after a year when traffic deaths were at a record nigh. Unless an indicator is in a period of permanent upward growth, chance alone should lead you to expect that the indicator will drop below the record the next year. In other words, any reform can be made to look good, something that we as reporters often fail to realize.

These are all examples of how reporters can better report other people's numbers. The other reason for learning how to count and measure is that there are lots of things that we can count and measure ourselves. Survey research is one of the best examples, but there are other things too.

Many investigative stories, for example, involve analysis of public records. We did a project in Philadelphia last year in which we analyzed more than a thousand criminal cases to find out where the flaws were in the criminal justice system. We used the same sort of computer analysis used in survey research. The unit of analysis was not an inter— view; it was a set of records about a particular criminal case.

To utilize these tools as reporters, you need to know just two things.You need a little bit of statistics and you need to know enough about computers to process your own data. Understanding the computer is fairly important. You do not have to do your own programming, but you should be able to at least talk to the computer programmer. If you learn how to handle the computer control cards yourself, you'll develop a nice sense of power, and will also find it easier to learn the statistics when you can go to the computer immediately and implement them. The electronic calculator helps a little but it's nothing like the computer. Computer programs are available which enable you to talk to the computer almost in plain English. We did a recent election survey in a Michigan congressional district in which we wanted to know which issues were the best predictor of a vote for the Democrat or the Republican. We found very quickly through a computer crosstabulation that the main issue was Watergate and the second most important issue was Nixon's taxes. The voters' general attitude toward the President was also a very high predictor.

We also wanted to know why the Michigan voters seemed to dislike President Nixon. Several hypotheses seemed

240

reasonable: the high cost of living, unemployment in the district, concern about farm prices, and, of course, Watergate. We simply told the computer to correlate each of these issues against attitude toward Nixon. We had asked our respondents to evaluate the importance of about a dozen major issues and to evaluate the performance of President Nixon on each of them. So we had continuous variables on which we could compute correlation coefficients. Then we did a multiple regression analysis in which we asked the computer in effect to tell us how much of the anti–Nixon attitude could be explained by Watergate and to tell us, once that variable is held constant, how much of the attitude could be explained by other variables.

What it told us was that the income tax issue had significant additional effect. That finding suggested that if the election hadn't been held the day after income taxes were due or if Nixon had not had his income tax problem that the Republican might have won the election––because it was that close. We also learned that after the effect of Watergate and income taxes was accounted for, no other issues predicted how people felt about the President. If a voter was unhappy with the President because of inflation or unemployment, that particular anger was already subsumed by the effect of Watergate or the income tax problem.

I was able to conduct this analysis myself, and the key instruction to the computer was simply one card that said, "Compute regressions." The computer is a powerful resource and more and more newspapers are beginning to realize they can do a lot of this analysis in house. This was the first time that we had used a computer at one of our own newspapers for a project of this nature. In Cincinnati we used the *Cincinnati Enquirer's* data processing department. That department was fast, efficient, and anxious to show it could do something for the newsroom. We were able to break down the traditional antipathy between the business and the editorial side of a newspaper. A project of this nature is costly but not out of sight. We did that Cincinnati survey for about $1,200––using my special accounting system. To estimate the cost of a project to an editor I measure costs in terms of the incremental value of a reporter's time. If I tell an editor a project will take four reporters for a week, he will say he can't spare them. To that I reply that the work they would have done is not lost because four other reporters who are almost as good will do what these four would have done. Furthermore the work that they would have done will not be lost because four other reporters, only somewhat less skilled can do that work. The rationale cycles down until all that has been sacrificed is the four least important stories done by the four least competent reporters. It works!

Smaller newspapers also are becoming interested in precision journalism. A journalism student called me recently before going to a job interview at a paper with a circulation of 30,000. One of the things the editor wanted in this new reporter was some capability for precision journalism projects. The student asked me to suggest some projects that a paper with a small budget could do.

Some medium–sized papers also are assigning people to do this on a more or less full–time basis. A modest–sized paper in Wilmington, Del., has a very sophisticated infor-

242

mation retrieval system which it used to trace patterns of dope dealing in the Wilmington area and which led to some major exposes on the narcotics and heroin racket.

Reporters can also tap some centralized data resources available throughout the country. Some of the new computer systems are interactive so that you can sit down at the keyboard, type out questions, and get answers in return. Some of these interactive systems can give you access to the results of election surveys stored at the University of Michigan. If you are writing an election story and want to know how many people were concerned about unemployment among the Wallace voters of 1968, you can get such data from Michigan through the terminal where you are working.

Likewise, you can get data from the General Social Survey done at the University of Chicago. That survey—a general purpose survey about social change—includes standardized questions about racial attitudes, attitudes toward women's liberation, political attitudes, and life style questions. And the survey repeats many of these questions from year to year. The purpose of this broad—scale survey is to provide data for people who don't have the money to sponsor their own surveys. The people who conduct the survey promise they will write nothing about it—no scholarly reports on it—until it has been in the public domain for at least one year. The code books and data cards are available at cost, or the data can be obtained from a centralized interactive system. If you have the right terminal and know the telephone number, you can call up the computer and say, ''What percentage of husbands are making their own breakfasts in 1974 as compared with 1975?

I have been asked to speculate about the future of precision journalism. Several years ago, before I knew that what I was doing was precision journalism, someone asked if this was the wave of the future. I said, "Well, maybe" and now I would say, "Yes, it probably is." The best sign is that small papers are doing it. Another encouraging sign is that big papers are hiring outside experts to do quantitative projects for them (which I really do not approve of because a reporter should not hire somebody else to do his thinking for him.) The reporter should have the skills himself so that his newspaper doesn't have to hire an expert to write a report about the report. It's better to do the research directly and more and more reporters are developing the necessary skills.

I think a reporter's ability to count is analogous to his ability to spell. A bright young reporter I knew on the Miami *Herald* in the 1950's was a lousy speller. His spelling was the pain of the copy desk, so one day the assistant managing editor called him over to his desk and said, "Tom, I want to talk to you about your spelling." Tom knew he was in trouble until Al Neuharth, the editor, said, "Every newspaper has got to have one guy who's a lousy speller, because if we don't have at least one lousy speller we don't have anybody to hold up as an example to everybody else in the city room. We need one guy who's spelling is so bad that when he walks by we can say to the rest of our reporters, "Look at that guy, he can't spell." Tom was feeling pretty good then. But Al said, "On this newspaper that man is Steve Trumball. You learn to spell!"

I foresee the day when a reporter will be called to the

244

city desk, and the city editor will say, "You learn to count!"

---

[1] Everette E. Dennis, *The Magic Writing Machine* (Eugene: School of Journalism, University of Oregon, 1971).

[2] Philip Meyer, *Precision Journalism* (Bloomington: Indiana University Press, 1973).

[3] Albert H. Cantril and Charles W. Roll, Jr., *Hopes and Fears of the American People* (New York: Universe Books: 1971).

15

THE FUTURE OF SCIENCE AND MEDICAL REPORTING

Victor Cohn

Science reporting is merely the application of the best tools of reporting——open eyes and a prepared mind——to the workings of science and technology. And science reporting is becoming more and more a necessity as the world becomes more and more technological. Science and technology rule our lives and produce swift and often devastating social change. If we are to survive, it is vital that we understand the events that portend social change. This is what science reporting is all about.

Almost since the dawning of science there have been scientists who wrote and spoke well about science. They are the great science popularizers, and they are still to be heard and seen, most strikingly lately on television in shimmering color. Science popularization is fascinating and important. But it is not the primary job of the science reporter, though many scientists think that it should be. A modern science reporter does more than describe science. He relates it to today's social, political and economic events.

This reporting style began in the United States at about the time of World War I. It was nurtured in the 1920s and 1930s by only a few dozen writers——Watson Davis, the

246

the founder of Science Service, William L. Laurence of the *New York Times*, David Dietz of Scripps—Howard and a handful of others.

Their kind of reporting grew slowly until an event over Hiroshima in 1945. Then a whole new crop of writers came back from World War II to our newspapers convinced that science was going to reshape the world and that someone ought to be writing about it. Those of us in this new crop spent a lot of time writing about atomic energy until gradually we broadened our interest to all of science. That same broadening process has happened over the years to space writers, environmental writers and is already happening to the new energy writers.

After Hiroshima, the ranks of science writers grew into the few hundreds. Then the launching of the first space satellite, the Soviet Sputnik, in the fall of 1947 captured the public mind and caused a vast reexamination of American capabilities in science, technology, and education. As Sputnik jarred the nation, interest in science reporting and the numbers of science writers reached a high point. Project Apollo and the years of exciting progress toward a moon landing continued the process.

But then we developed other concerns. We had turned toward outer space at the price of neglect of the earth. The realization that we were living in a deteriorating environment, our awareness of being caught in a terrible web of growing population, growing need for resources and growing dependence on ever more complex technologies which seem to further threaten both our environment and our freedom—— all these things have made many people say, "What good is science?" And many editors have wearied of still another

247

story about a new nuclear particle or neutron star.

In short, in the last few years, editors and the public have shown less interest in some of the old kinds of science, even though the new concern with energy has given science writing a shot in the arm. People have become disenchanted with some of the products of science and therefore disenchanted with hearing about science. David Perlman of the *San Francisco Chronicle* noted last year that "among the nation's 1,750 daily newspapers and two major wire services, there are fewer than 75 full—time science writers all told," and there is "virtually no biology, no behavioral science, no physical science on everyday television."

True enough. But I think we have been passing through a low point and things may be improving. Under the talented Earl Ubell, a longtime science reporter now a TV news director, WNBC—TV in New York City is doing first—class daily science news reporting. One of the major networks at the moment I write this is looking for a full—time science reporter, who, with ABC's capable pioneer, Jules Bergman, may create the beginning of a corps of science reporters on national networks, probably influencing future local TV reporters.

The TV science specials, especially the BBC's, are also getting very good. American TV is exploring a number of imaginative ways of reporting the progress and problems of medicine. And the entertainment shows like "Marcus Welby, M.D." and "Emergency" are doing a good deal of interesting medical reporting. In short, I don't disagree with Perlman on the deficiencies of the Vast Wasteland; in fact, I'd go further. But it's not quite the whole story.

248

As to newspapers, on the day I first gave this presentation I picked up a current issue of the *New York Times*, the March 25, 1974, edition, and checked off the stories about science, technology and medicine. On page one: "It has been found that dogs can be used successfully where human therapists have failed in treating certain forms of schizophrenia." And throughout the paper: "The oldest moon rock has been found to be 4.5 billion years old." By the Pentagon reporter: "Landmark nuclear pact up for review." On the business page: "Shale oil search intensifies in reaction to Arab action." On what used to be called the Women's Page: "Civil rights of mental patients debated by medical and legal professions." Also from Washington: "More in U.S. rely on sterilization." "Expert opposes new nerve gases." "Gains in cancer program are hailed." "The city museum offers a multimedia VD exhibit." Even a review of a new book by Bruno Bettelheim on home treatment of autistic children.

In the next day's *Times* I found a report on research about behavior and violence, a finding that carbon monoxide in polluted air and cigarette smoke can bring on pain in hardened arteries, a report on cancer and diet, a Washington story on nuclear power plant hearings, and reviews of TV programs on cancer, Vitamin E and childbirth. Finally, there was an analytical piece about methadone and heroin deaths.

Most of these stories were written by science and medical reporters and they appeared on just two days. Most *but not all* were written by science reporters. And this is another reason why it is unrealistic today to assess the state of science reporting merely by counting science reporters.

Now that the proliferation of nuclear power plants has become a diplomatic, economic, *and* military issue, at least two diplomatic reporters and the Pentagon reporter on the *Washington Post* today frequently write and write well about nuclear technology; not only military technology but also civilian technology. The same reporters possess expert knowledge of missilery.

The business and economics writers have had to learn a good deal about the technology of energy. Our Moscow correspondent has to know about space, missile and nuclear matter and our correspondents in other capitals face up to similar demands. And they do so in much better fashion than they'd have done 20 years ago.

In other words, specialization on newspapers has advanced to the point where it is no longer the province of the specialist alone. The first—class newspaper today expects its reporters in general to possess the education and prepared minds to become instant experts if need be, and I for one find it very exciting to watch a stream of young, generalist reports meeting this demand with vast ability and energy.

Another example that comes to mind out of today's headlines: our leading court reporter on the *Post* had to learn about abortions and the fetus to cover the Supreme Court decisions, then the Edelin trial. This knowledge is now another arrow in his quiver, and the same is true of scores of subjects. You used to hear it said by the old—timers decisions on abortion and to caver the Edelin trial related to the ''death'' of a fetus after an abortion. This knowledge is now another arrow in his quiver, and the same is true of of subjects. You used to hear it said by the old—timers

250

when I was a young reporter that "any reporter can cover any story." That was never true, or it was never true that *any* reporter could cover any story *well*. Yet it is much closer to truth today.

What I am trying to say is that science reporters do not and should not own science. And it is a healthy thing that science is more a part of the general body of knowledge (and maybe just some of us graying science reporters can claim a small shred of credit.)

Certainly, some kinds of science reporting have been in decline but perhaps not quite as much as some people think. We are without doubt now in an era in which the word "science" no longer automatically sends a chill through an editor's veins. At the same time, no conscious decision is made that "today we're going to cover some science," but traher the press of events——like abortion debates, Edelin trials and fetal research controversies——*demand* informed coverage.

Some of this can and must be done by other kinds of reporters. But when a President or a leading candidate or a senator is shot and editors suddenly need a medical account on zero minute's notice, they look for a medical reporter. I can think of many instances on the *Washington Post* in recent years when a science or medical reporter has sudden—ly been called on to write——say, at 5 o'clock for a 7 o'clock deadline——on unexpected notice of the artificial synthesis of the gene, or an environmental disaster, or new evidence for a cancer virus.

The crush of such events demands a prepared interpreter. News is a fast–breaking, competitive and perishable commo—dity, and making the first edition with a late–breaking science or medical story calls for a reporter with ready access to knowledgeable sources, a stack of reliable and

251

familiar reference works and above all a bank of knowledge in his mind.

When I worked on the *Minneapolis Tribune* from the 1940's through the 1960's, John Cowles, the remarkable owner, often said that a first class reporter should know as much about his field as a Ph.D. or professor in the field. That was a rare statement for a newspaper publisher then or now. His ideal was in truth impossible for a reporter of science and technology because he would have to know a hundred fields, not just one. Yet a science reporter can and should know the vocabulary and highlights and general issues and some of the important questions to ask in a large number of fields, as well as the general spirit and the rules of scientific inquiry, which apply anyplace.

A difficult and challenging goal? Of course. Science writing is fresh and exciting because it is ever challenging. Something new and unexpected is almost always happening. Every few years a new field demands telling.

The science reporter of today who would keep science reporting alive also has to be alert to opportunities to add his special points of view and expertise to many kinds of running stories. Take Watergate and all it still implies.

Watergate was a story of the misuse of electronics. Citizens and scientists had been warning for the past 25 or 30 years of two related dangers: the subversion of government by science and the subversion of science by government. The revelations of Watergate told us that both were happening.

Time noted that agents like G. Gordon Liddy and E. Howard Hunt "set out with zest and technological skill and

252

a mind boggling indifference to the Bill of Rights." Unfortunately for them and fortunately for society, they didn't have enough technological skill. Yet the technology used at the Watergate Office Building pales when we consider the possibilities of eavesdropping by supersensitive, long distance listening devices or by bouncing a laser beam off a window to pick up conversations from the mere vibrations on the glass. The difference between coming electronic technologies and Watergate technology will be like the difference between the long bow and the A—bomb.

Similarly, the crude break—in of the office of Daniel Ellsberg's psychiatrist seems almost a minor event when we consider that health insurance companies are already putting medical information on policy holders into computer memory banks and exchanging such information through a central repository. How long will it be before anyone with the right code will have access to our medical histories? Even well-meant safeguards may have little effect against a criminal with sophisticated electronic tools. We are in a growing era of computerized personnel records, credit records, criminal histories and arrest records, all obtainable at the touch of a keyboard at any of thousands of terminals. Science reporters should be among those who are reporting this accelerating trend toward an impersonal and technologically equipped government, made seemingly inevitable by a growing population and rapidly advancing methodologies.

Science writers should be and are writing about coming advances in biology and genetics and the onrush of genetic testing and engineering. Forgive a personal example, but a few years ago I began to look into the then year—or—so—old

253

federal crusade against sickle cell anemia. I discovered to my amazement that several states as well as the District of Columbia had passed laws calling for *compulsory* sickle cell anemia screening of blacks, for example, school children. These were the country's first compulsory genetic screening laws aimed at a single racial group, a very, very, large screen to pick up a small number of people, and their enactment and imminent application had gone largely unreported. I found that people in the black community were deeply disturbed about these laws. Most geneticists, I found, feel that people should be screened for genetic diseases *if* they want to be screened. But they also feel that there ought to be a good deal of public debate, which there had not been in the sickle cell case, before we enact any compulsory testing, especially testing designed to convince certain people not to have children.

These sickle cell laws had been on the books for a year or more, yet nobody had collected and reported all the pertinent facts. I wrote a series on sickle cell anemia, which was followed by articles in the *Saturday Review* and *Newsweek* and other publications. The states involved soon repealed or modified or ignored their screening laws. The *Washington Post* can't claim all the credit, but I think that our series helped. I also think there are hundreds of similar opportunities out in the political, societal and scientific woods, hanging on the trees for the alert reporter to harvest.

Of course, medical and health reporting always has been the bread and butter of science writing. A science writer on the Associated Press once supposedly said that he could get a story on the front page of every one of AP's 2,500

254

member newspapers if he wrote about ulcers, piles or sexual impotence, three ailments which he said every editor either has or thinks he might get. Medical reporting is popular, and it's exciting. It is also easily abused——by inaccuracy, exaggeration or irresponsibility. Or the pressure that we all feel to make today's story budget, today's news show, today's front page.

Arthur J. Snider of the *Chicago Daily News* once wrote that "the record would show that 90 per cent of the stories we have written about new drugs have gone down the drain as failures." I find that I wrote 10 years ago that: "I think we all know this. We know that false hopes fill doctors' offices with sufferers who must be disappointed. We must report the truly important, but we need to show more dis—crimination and moderation, and include qualifications early in the story. We need to know more about interpreting, and sometimes questioning, statistics. So do doctors——and scientists. They give us the news in the first place." All of this is still true.

I——with others——also wrote then: "We over—use a bagful of cliches, like 'major breakthrough' and 'giant step forward.' I quote Turner Catledge: 'We have worn out our superlatives; we have spent our emotions; we have exhausted our imagination in the search for the exciting.' ...(And) Dr. Polykarp Kusch: 'The reader is bombarded by news of the new triumphs of science but fails to understand that even science has its limitations.' Science is not just a series of breakthroughs but a long, hard, and today, expensive search."

"We science writers, except for an exceptional few, fail

255

to pay enough attention to basic research, and we too often fire out news of new discoveries, or what we call discoveries, without connecting them with the main body of knowledge and the basic work that has gone before.''

"We are not well enough educated. We   need mainly generalists, people with both a liberal education *and* science to report science. But more of us could spend far more time learning more. The National Association of Science Writers created, to this end, the Council for the Advancement of Science Writing, and the council has been taking some good steps in this direction. So have others. We need to   take more; I think our present brief seminars need to grow into bona fide postgraduate courses which writers take period-ically in the same way that conscientious doctors continue to study.''

All these things are still true. But there has been im-provement. Far more science   writers are coming to the field with a generous dose of scientific education. There is less concern with the latest candidate for leading cancer virus (though this will change and our naivete will return as soon as someone appears to truly find one!), and there is a far   larger corps if not of science   writers in sheer numbers, rather than of sophisticated science writers who better learned how to meet the requirements of daily output without insulting the facts and spirit of science.

I don't want to sound over–stuffy. I think we are still primarily newsmen. At his recent retirement dinner after a long and bright career with the Associated Press, Frank Carey told of participating in a symposium some years ago with Jack McKelway of the *Washington Evening Star*, at a

256

time when the *Star* was Washington's leading newspaper and McKelway was for a time its medical reporter. The reporters at the symposium were asked to give their answers to the question, "What is legitimate medical news?" McKelway said, "Gentlemen, my definition of legitimate medical news is news that appears in the *Washington Star* before it appears in the *Washington Post.*"

Amen. But it's got to be right. And we ought to know enough now to throw it out if it's statistically outrageous. And if we don't understand the statistical tests ourselves, we ought to know where to ask, and that we *should* ask. It is encouraging that the Council for the Advancement of Science Writing has helped take the lead in training general reporters and editors in the new technique of what Phil Meyer, its Moses, calls "precision journalism," that is, applying statistical sampling and computer technology to reporting.

This is long overdue. At the same time, let's not quit using our legs. Take the great portion of today's medical story sometimes called "health economics." The economics and organization of medical care are going to be a major and continuing story for many years. Broadened health insurance is already resulting in new controls, new ways of delivery and new emphasis on the quality of medical care.

I think the press has had a good deal of trouble in properly telling the changing health care story. It is an amorphous, difficult, technical and often secretive area. Not surprisingly, therefore, it is often covered poorly.

The place where the news media have done best—— though at best still only a fair job——is in covering the big health picture. By this I mean the fact that the United States is still the only modern state which has not learned to spread the costs of health care with at least some degree of justice, or to make health care at least generally accessible to all its people. I mean the fact that while doctors are generally sincere and compassionate and dedicated people, far too many have been seduced into money grubbing by the present system. I mean the fact that the cost of care has escalated so greatly that congress is frightened today of financing a really thorough national health insurance system.

The press is doing at least a fair job of presenting this big health picture. Where we are lax is in revealing the little picture. We focus on the AMA, HEW, Congress, even city and state policies and programs. But we don't yet spend much time in the hospitals, the clinics, the doctors' offices, those places where the best and worst in health care are given.

In Minneapolis and St. Paul there is a remarkable old-fashioned newspaperman named Paul Presbrey, old-fashioned in the best sense, a one—man army who always carried a little black notebook about the size of a pocket bible and wore dark and funeral clothes which made him look like a minister whenever there was a disaster. He would stick this notebook over his chest like a Bible and never had any trouble getting into a hospital to get the story.

I think this is how a great many of us need to be using our legs to get into the places where the health care is delivered. I spent my first four years at the *Washington Post* largely covering science, space, and science policy. Then, because I had suggested it when I came to the newspaper and because I was reminded of the suggestion by a remark—

able managing editor, I began to look at Virginia suburbs. The community hospital, not the cyclotron, is where science meets the people. And the opportunities there are rich and ripe.

For example, one of our investigative reporters, Ronald Kessler, spent four months producing a series of articles on conflicts of interests between hospitals and business. The hospital series focused mainly on the Washington Hospital Center——Washington's largest community hospital, affiliated with universities and widely respected. Through an enormous amount of hard work he uncovered the fact that trustees and officers of this hospital were officials of banks and businesses dealing with the hospital, often at high cost to the patients and the health insurance—paying public.

Two administrators of the hospital had formed a computer calculating company with a $50,000 advance from the hospital; the company then got the payroll and accounting contract from the hospital. One trustee was the president of a stockbroking firm which handled the hospital's $4.5 million pension plan. The young broker responsible for buying and selling stocks for the pension fund was the son—in—law of a trustee who headed the bank which handled the hospital's large and then interest—free accounts.

Kessler found that 10 of the hospital's 38 trustees had serious conflicts of interest. He learned from the Social Security Administration, Blue Cross, hospital accounting firms, and American Hospital Association officials that such practices were common in hospitals and that they needed to be corrected. Some major changes have been made at this hospital and others since.

About a year later, I began looking into a controversy over the proposed building of a hospital on Wisconsin Avenue in northwest Washington, a hospital which a good many people thought was not needed. My own doctor, a good friend, was the leader of the group of 50 doctors who wanted to build this hospital. I ultimately learned that in the territory within a 35—mile radius of the Department of Health, Education and Welfare, which is supposed to be the nation's center of health planning, more than $500 million was being spent or was about to be spent on new hospitals or additions without one hour ever having been spent on area—wide planning. In the opinion of Blue Cross and other officials about half of this spending was unnecessary.

Most of these building plans came about because of local pride, misguided views of health needs, local business zest and conflicts of interest, and other wrong—minded, narrow or plainly selfish reasons. The public was being told that this or that new hospital "will not cost you a cent to build," because the hospital was going up without government aid. But the claim was always a lie because almost every cent of the money to build every hospital ultimately has to come from the public through Blue Cross, insurance, Medicare and Medicaid payments.

In effect, the Washington metropolitan area, in the shadow of the nation's capital, had the worst hospital planning of any area in the United States. The lack of planning was costing the people of this area millions of dollars in increased health insurance premiums and hospital bills, money that could well have been spent to meet other crucial needs. We printed all this, and many follow—up stories, and this has been doing some good in the year and a half since in

260

killing off some bad projects and getting some planning started.

The whole situation––the unneeded building, the bad or non–existent planning, the gross waste of public money–– all were just the kind of situation that *any* reporter who gets out of the office and talks to the people on the beat can't help bumping into. Every newspaper today needs a health reporter who, if you'll forgive the phrase, knows where the bodies are buried. Too much of medical reporting has been the easy kind of reporting of discoveries, breakthroughs, and abnormalities which we soak up from medical journals and medical meetings. Sitting at county commissioners' business sessions and public meetings where citizens argue until midnight about some minor project, in the national view, is far more time–consuming and tedious. But it is the only way a reporter can get the whole health picture.

Dr. Osler Peterson of the Harvard School of Public Health some years ago had his students sit in doctors' offices to observe the quality of medical care provided to patients. The results were eye–opening. Health reporters need to do the same kind of observing if they are to under– stand health care as the doctor–patient relationship that it is.

Many new practices are just beginning in health care–– peer review, hospital auditing, quality control. Some of them will go well, some of them will go badly. We need people to audit the auditors and peer at the peer reviewers. Reporters will have to get at the real core of the news by reading aud– its, attending clinics, and talking to doctors and patients. Yes, and not just guessing at facts but applying some of

Phil Meyer's precision, computer journalism.

Then, as health care and health insurance broaden, we may be able to help prevent some of the unnecessary surgery, errors in prescribing medication, poor quality care, ineffectual drugs, and high infection rates. We are rapidly heading into a vast new national experiment in mass health care delivery, but the experiment will really consist of thousands of small ones in thousands of hospitals and medical centers. It is up to the future health reporter to help tell us not only which of these are not working but which are working and where, so others can learn and improve the end product, which will be everyone's health.

Many other things could be said about science and medical reporting, but one more must be said. Science reporting is also fun. It is a share in the scientific adventure of Galileo, Copernicus, Darwin, Einstein, Pasteur, Salk and Sabin and the white—coated medical practitioner trying something new to save a life in the hospital down the road.

Good science reporters know that when you walk through hosptial corridors and look in on laboratories you run across stories. Then you can both make the front page and help people understand our new complex kind of news.

16

CHANGES IN SCIENCE REPORTING

Sharon M. Friedman

In the last several years, science and technology have been criticized for their lack of application to national needs, for their deleterious effects on the natural environment, and for their use or misure by the military. Funding for basic research has decreased, the job market for researchers has been shrinking, and fewer students want to study science in high schools and colleges.

Things were different in 1965.[1] That was the golden time—the space program was booming, funding levels were climbing toward their all—time high of $17 billion in fiscal 1968, and the public seemed optimistic about science.

What caused this change was a complex interaction of events at both the national and international levels. In an effort to pin down one aspect of the changes, a nationwide study[2] was launched in 1973 to determine whether methods for communicating news of science[3] to the public had changed since 1965,[4] and whether the kind of person seeking a career in science writing had changed. Investigators were primarily interested in how suspected changes in science writing could affect the public's attitudes toward science.

Based on information obtained from 17 in—depth interviews with science writers in December 1972, an eight—page questionnaire was prepared and mailed to active members of the National Association of Science Writers (NASW) in April 1973. Usable surveys were returned by 153 writers—a 40 percent return rate. Others sent in letters and explanatory notes. The survey returns appear to be highly representative of the active membership of NASW in most demographic variables, including age, sex, geographic location, education levels, and media representation.

CHANGES IN SCIENCE WRITING

Three major changes appear to have occurred in science writing since 1965. There is an increasing emphasis on presenting information that is relevant to the reader. Interpretative reporting is on the rise. And science is being presented to the public in a more unfavorable light. In addition, a number of changes have occurred in such areas as content, coverage determinants, and amount of space given to science by publications.

Science stories that simply stir the reader's imagination are giving way to stories that contain information a reader might find useful in daily life. When asked what makes a good science story, the greatest number of writers—more than a fourth—cited relevance of the story to the reader as their top criterion. Said one writer: "There is an emphasis away

264

from cold, indifferent science to that which produces some gain in the quality of life.''

This attitude is reflected in the change in subject matter. Most writers believed that stories on outer space received the most media coverage in 1965, followed by stories on health and medicine. In 1973, environmental issues, as well as health and medicine, were perceived as paramount. Essentially, space articles, which caught the imagination of many in the mid–1960's, have been replaced by topics that hit closer to home.

About half of the writers answering the survey indicated they wrote more interpretative[5] than straight news[6] articles on science. A quarter of the writers said they wrote more straight news stories, while the remainder wrote equal amounts of both types. Since more interpretative stories on science are written for scientific and medical publications than for newspapers, an analysis was made of answers from newspaper writers alone: almost twice as many wrote more interpretative pieces on science than wrote straight news articles.

Said one writer: "The gee whiz story has taken a back seat to interpretative pieces that view science as a pro–cess.''Another pointed out a "growing conviction that public understanding requires lucidity and interpretative expla–nation.''

Because science writers are writing on more relevant topics, they must necessarily deal with controversial issues. Examining both the pros and the cons of issues frequently puts science in a worse light than did articles typical of 1965. Nine years ago, the mood was optimistic: readers

265

were made to feel that science was good for them and that it was the way of the future.

Inevitably, with today's emphasis on science's mistakes as well as its virtues, even science writers themselves are more distrustful of their subjects than they once were. Over two—thirds said they were more inclined to question information given then by science sources than they had been in 1965. Almost half indicated that from one—fourth to more than one—half of their articles could be perceived by their readers as being unfavorable to science.

CHANGES IN SCIENCE WRITERS

Have science writers changed enough since 1965 to effect changes in the profession? Most survey respondents seemed to think so, pointing out increases in the number of writers and in the importance of their role. They felt that science writers are better educated and more sophisticated than they were in 1965 and that they increasingly act as watchdogs over science.

Another, perhaps more important, factor emerged: Younger science writers (age 20 to 30) differ in a number of ways from their older colleagues (age 31 and over). For example, the younger writers have better training in science, with almost half of them[7] having majored in science in under—graduate school. Only one fifth of the older writers did so.

Nearly half of the older science writers indicated they became interested in science writing while working on a publication. Only a few had pursued it as a career goal while in school. In contrast, almost half of the younger writers had training in science writing, either in undergraduate or graduate school. Less than a tenth went into science writing after having worked on a publication.

Three quarters of the younger writers specialize in the fields they cover compared to three fifths of the older writers, and they are more concerned with reader relevance. Citing this factor as the most important coverage determinant were more than half of the younger writers compared to only one fifth of the rest of the group. Whether these differences will continue after the younger writers have been in the profession for some time is uncertain. Yet it does seem probable that these younger writers exemplify a new breed that will significantly reshape science writing.

THE EFFECT OF PUBLIC OPINION

The second factor identified by the science writers as causing changes in the profession was a shift in public attitudes about science. The writers perceived that public attitudes today are far more negative than they were in 1965, and they believed that the Vietnam War and environmental concerns were the two elements most responsible.

About one—third of the writers said their own attitudes or writing styles had been affected by unfavorable public attitudes toward science, and more than two—thirds believed these negative attitudes on the part of the public had af—

fected science and technology. Funding cuts were seen as a major result of public attitudes.

There appears to be interaction between the attitudes of certain segments of the public and science writers. Along with other factors, this interaction has contributed to a general skepticism and dissatisfaction with science in today's society. Although in the short term this development may bode ill, in the long term it may be a blessing in disguise. For the public, it could provide a more realistic view of science. For science, it could create a more respon-sible attitude toward applications of research. For science writing, it already seems to be reorienting the profession from the "gee whizzers" of yesterday to the more thoughtful interpreters and critics of today, who see and treat science as a major and inseparable part of current society.[8]

---

[1] J. L. Penick et al., Eds., *The Politics of American Science, 1939 to the Present* (Cambridge. Mass.: MIT Press, 1972). p.331.

[2] A portion of this study was supported by a grant from the Office of Communications Programs for the Public Understanding of Science of the American Association for the Advancement of Science. Logistic assistance was provided by the National Association of Science Writers: the School of Journalism at The Pennsylvania State Uni-versity, through its *Reader's Digest* Student Research and Travel Grant; and the College of Liberal Arts and Penn-

sylvania Field Research Laboratory at Penn State.

[3] Science was defined in the questionnaire to include technology, as well as pure and applied research in the biological, physical, medical, behavioral, and environmental areas.

[4] Although the year 1965 is cited as the baseline year for this study, the period from 1965 through 1968 was actually used in the questionnaire for this purpose in order to avoid answers based on specific events in each year.

[5] Interpretative articles were defined in the questionnaire "as either those that focus on how an aspect of science affects the public, or those that provide a perspective or assessment of the status of a scientific area. Emphasizing explanation, these articles also include some factual reporting."

[6] Straight news articles were defined in the questionnaire "as those that report the happenings of science with little explanation of how these events affect the public or fit into a larger perspective."

[7] The number of persons in this younger writer category remains constant at 5 throughout the study. Although this number is small, it is representative of the number of writers of this age that are members of the National Association of Science Writers. Six additional writers in this age group were interviewed as part of the survey done in December 1972. While their answers are not included in the national survey data, they correspond to those reported for their age category and reinforce the findings.

[8] Data for this article comes from a Master's Thesis in preparation for the School of Journalism at Pennsylvania State University.

17

REPORTING THE FUTURE AND THE FUTURE
OF SPECIALIZED REPORTING

Jonathan Ward

If the entire 4.7 billion year history of the earth—moon system were squeezed into the six biblical days of creation, the first life on the planet would have appeared Tuesday night at eleven. By half past noon on Saturday the first spiders would appear. About suppertime the great dinosaurs would appear and at 9:50 they would vanish. The hominid that would become man shows up about five minutes before midnight Saturday. Peking man, and woman no doubt, would be trying to keep their fires going at a minute before twelve. Neanderthal man would be burying his dead with flowers six seconds before the new day. Two seconds before Sunday bison were frozen in paintings on a cave wall in what, a fifth of a second before twelve, became the Republic of France. Nine thousandths of a second before the new day R. Buckminster Fuller was born.

It is now midnight according to my time scheme. Take a seventh day for rest. The eighth day is the future.

The future is a funny thing. It doesn't seem to be just a past that hasn't happened yet. It seems more open somehow. The past seems to be as real and as set as a painting on a cave wall. The future seems to radiate out from this present like the ribs of a Japanese fan——ribs of possibility——a fan of alternatives.

270

If you accept that analogy, that makes a futurist, one who deals with the future, a fan dancer. However, the thought of 300–pound Herman Kahn as a fan dancer is enough to give you an itch in your imagination.

For three years or so I have followed the Futurists. On the wings of my CBS expense account I traveled from the Rand Corporation in Santa Monica to the Institute for the Future and the Stanford Research Institute, both in Menlo Park, to the Hudson Institute in upstate New York to the Futures Group in Glastonbury, Connecticut. I visited Isaac Asimov at the Oliver Cromwell Hotel and Arthur C. Clarke, who commutes from Sri Lanka, at the Chelsea Hotel. I met a scientist who wanted to breed a race of mindless human beings to use as spare parts––I met a biologist who is convinced that we can, through careful genetic manipulation, create a living breathing unicorn. I met a talking computer and one that could sing. In trying to report on the future I have read some of the most ponderous prose that man has ever created––essays on the Post Industrial Society that were not so much written as hacked from the language. I've learned how to construct a morphology tree, how to use cross impact matrix analysis, how to conduct a Delphi study. While I can't talk to a computer in any machine language stronger than Basic, I have some sense of computer mod–eling. And I understand why the members of the Club of Rome are worried.

I'm not looking for a medal.

The future is a good beat. If you're reporting predictions of events sufficiently far off, you can be safely dead before anyone can check to see if you had the facts right. A fact in

271

the future is not the same thing as a fact in the present. If you predict the death of mankind because of air pollution, for example, your prediction is circulated widely, people become concerned, laws are passed, and air pollution does not wipe out mankind. Your statement about the future was wrong. Science fiction writer Ray Bradbury said once, "I write about the future not to predict it, but to prevent it." A futurist must intend to be wrong.

There's another problem with the future. Human beings seem to become nervous if they feel that they are predictable. Abraham Maslow talks about a girl in grade school who passed out french fries instead of test papers one day. She was normally well—behaved but she was tired of her good behavior being taken for granted. You can call this the court jester syndrome. For human beings rationality isn't every—thing. Predictability isn't all that desirable. For every Judge Hoffman there's an Abbie Hoffman. For every Dick Nixon, a Dick Tuck.

I mentioned some of the tools the futurists use——and I think that area is another problem. Morphology trees—— glorified decision charts——were constructed by the Stanford Reseach people for the most part. Cross impact techniques ——where several predictions are played off against each other——are used at the Institute for the Future and a spin—off think tank the Futures Group. The Rand Corporation was quite involved with Delphi questionnaires——which is a little more than a polling of experts with feedback aiming at group consensus.

Incidentally, I have a Delphi questionaire on my desk now. It's designed to reveal the future of...Delphi ques-

tionnaires .It makes me nervous. There's something inces-
tuous about that study.

Computer modeling seems to work fairly well when your
primary task is number crunching. CBS at one time had a
model of the financial aspects of a film company on its
computer. It could tell you what would happen to the profit
picture if the cost of processing film went up a penny a
foot. It could not predict that a movie about demonic pos-
session was the way to get a profit picture in the first place.

So now we have three problems with reporting the future:
1. A prediction can't take into account its own existence.
So the really juicy forecasts——the truly bone chilling
predictions——the ones that make good copy——are probably
wrong .
2. People just don't want to be predictable——to be a cog
in the futurists' machine. They'll foul up your grand plan
every chance they get.
3. The techniques the futurists use just aren't that useful
and they are over applied. You could call it the law of the
tool——when all you have is a hammer everything looks like
a nail.

Then there's the sheer complexity of trying to do technological or social assessment. I talked to a man from
Arthur D. Little Incorporated of Cambridge, Massachusetts,
a think tank that does proprietary research. He was a specialist in modular housing so I asked some innocuous
questions about the future of housing in the United States.
He said:

"Listen, Sonny. I can turn out modular housing units by
the millions. I can build a machine that will spit out three

273

complete houses a minute. I can make houses out of spun spinach or compressed bus tickets. But first tell me how I change the building codes to allow the houses to be built, and tell me how I find financing for my research and development work, and tell me how I stabilize mortgage rates so that people can afford to buy houses, and tell me where I can find decent communities that have room for my houses—— then I'll talk to you about the future of housing." Or take another case.

Let's say you are interviewing Robert C. W. Ettinger—— a perfectly pleasant older man who happens to be fascinated with cryonic burial. He thinks that we should freeze our dead. We should pack them away in liquid nitrogen and wait for the day when we can cure not only the disease that killed them—but the effects of the cold storage. If you suggest that the prospect seems unlikely——he argues that with his method there is at least some chance of living again. With standard burial techniques there is zero chance. To do the proper job on the subject you can't drop it there. You have to check with a lawyer to see how he would settle the estate of someone in suspended animation. You'd have to check with a marriage counsellor to see if the spouse of the semi—departed was free to marry again. I talked to a psychologist who thought cryonic burial was a terrible idea. Death causes grief and grief is an essential psychological process. He didn't see how there could be grief over a person stored in a giant thermos bottle and he felt there would be all sorts of psychological difficulties later.

A social worker would want to know what this latter day Rip Van Winkle is going to do with himself after he wakes to a time that has no need of his skills. A banker
274

would be interested in the sleeper's modest savings account which as interest compounded over a century or so could grow to equal the gross national product of the free world.

A person in suspended animation could bankrupt the social security system. A life insurance agent would have to decide whether or not to pay off.

Can Medicaid be used to pay for suspended animation or is the technique to become a privilege of the rich?

Let's try another scenario——one where a minion of the law decides to determine whether or not there was foul play committed. Perhaps the sleeper wasn't legally dead in which case the undertaker who froze him can be charged with murder. The only way to decide that is for the coroner to conduct an autopsy. Can the coroner be sued for violating our corpse–sickle's civil rights——conducting an autopsy that would prevent any chance of resurrection.

And speaking of resurrection——how is Billy Graham going to take all this. He looks for an end to the world and the second coming of Christ in the fairly near future. When the sleeper is gathered up for the last judgment does he stand with those who were alive for apocalypse——or does he stand with the dead brought again to life?

What started out to be interesting speculation——a piece of technology suitable for Sunday supplements suddenly blossoms into a socio–economic–religio–legal problem. You come away from such a reporting job with two conclusions:

1. Everything is connected to everything else and
2. It's probably better that many are cold but few are frozen.

275

Is there any point to all this? I think so. The winds of change have become a whole gale and events are piling up outside the door like leaves. Some of those events have consequences that could be unpleasant or even fatal. Herman Kahn once collected accidents——events that could possibly wipe out life on earth. Nuclear war was on the list——but so was an increase in atmospheric particulate matter that would darken the air causing more heat to collect around the earth melting the ice caps and eventually cooking us. Kahn collected a hundred of these jolly little surprises. He figured that the odds of any one of them happening was 100 to one——but since he had a hundred of them...

Reporting the future can work as long as you're serving as an interface between the technical world——and the real people. But a futurist—reporter has to remember not to take himself too seriously. The futurists fall into that trap a lot. J. B. S. Haldane said once that the universe is not only queerer than we imagine——it's queerer than we *can* imagine. The future works that way too.

I was asked to talk about reporting the future and the future of specialized reporting. For the first part of it——so long as you change *the* future to futures, plural, I think it can be done and that it's important. I'd like to see a resident futurist——a good one——on staff in newsrooms. He would have to be backed up with a computing facility and a publications budget that would allow him to do serious trend spotting and analysis. We insist on using up great chunks of air time with weather forecasters and their silly maps—— why not have a forecaster forecaster who could say the equivalent of:

276

"A major depression over Washington will be moving to Wall Street in the next couple of days causing storms to develop in the boardrooms of Detroit."

That's unfortunately, only a little facetious.

Last week the New York State legislature voted down a bill that would have allowed drugstores to display openly contraceptive devices. A trend analyst, knowing America's historical attitude toward sex, knowing that teenagers make up the only segment of our population with a rising birthrate, might predict that young people would be most affected by the legislature's vote.

If the trend analyst was a broadcaster he might get two and a half minutes of air time. If he wrote for the *New York Daily News,* the same story would be illustrated with a three column picture of the woman who sponsored the bill... and the headline "Legislatrix wishes Plymouth Rock had Landed on the Pilgrims." The *Wall Street Journal* would run the story on the front page under the head "Puritan Smirk Ethic Alive in Albany."

Yes, I think there can be effective, interesting, morally defensible reporting of alternative futures. Part two of the title: The future of specialty reporting. Let's talk first about mass media, then we can talk about specialty reporting.

We've discovered recently that it's handy to have a lawyer—journalist on staff. Business reporters, science editors, sports specialists have long been gainfully employ-ed in the mass media. I would love to have a CPA—journalist on staff that could be turned loose on the books of oil companies. It would probably also help to have a burglar—

journalist on the staff to obtain copies of the books of the oil companies.

It's not the business reporter's daily averages, nor the lawyer—reporter's interpretation of statute, nor even the futurist—reporter's recitation of tomorrow's problems and possibilities that will be the mainstay of journalism in the future. Tomorrow's journalist will have the same specialty today's journalist has——people . We *all* have a vested interest in the future because we're all going to spend the rest of our lives there. All of us. Expert and non. Scientists and stoned out hippie. The specialists shall not inherit the earth...Thus saith the Ward.

18

CONSUMER REPORTING:

TOWARDS PROTECTING CONSUMERS

Francis Pollack

Upton Sinclair may still be turning in his grave, but consumer coverage is improving.

"You cannot get anything into the newspapers that in any way rubs against the business policy of the banks and department stores..."

–Upton Sinclair, quoting an editor in *The Brass Check* (1919)

It may be unreasonable to blame the messenger for the bad news he delivers, but more blame is reasonable when he withholds delivery. Critics of the press, from Upton Sinclair on, have blamed the news media for failing to deliver news about the latest outrages of the marketplace.

The terms of the accusation are fairly familiar by now: since the news media are dependent on advertising revenues, they cannot deliver the information the public needs to shop wisely.

An examination of current consumer reporting does not completely dispel such charges. Yet there is some dramatic evidence of improvement; perhaps we are on the threshold of a genuine change for the better. Consider some of the following recent developments:

—No less than a dozen papers and stations have courted the wrath of supermarket advertisers by recently reporting, by store name, the results of laboratory analyses of ground beef. In many instances, the meat was so bad (often containing unacceptable levels of fecal bacteria) that it constituted a health hazard.

—There are now, according to *Media & Consumer,* no fewer than 500 full—time consumer reporters in the nation's news media, a tenfold increase since Consumers Union made its first count in 1970. There are even some consumer editors. One of then, the *New York Times's* Gerald Gold, has been given broad responsibilities for bringing consumer consciousness to the paper's news and specialized sections: this has not gone unnoticed at other major papers and stations.

—The fuel crisis has acted as a catalyst for consumer journalism: today, most news organizations are sharply questioning the major oil companies.

280

—Some advertisers caught playing fast and loose with the public are getting much rougher treatment from the news media than they might ever have believed possible. Nelson Poynter, publisher of the St. Petersburg *Times and Evening Independent,* bounced a $235,000—a—year advertiser when his reporters discovered that the advertiser, an appliance dealer, was not only guilty of bait and switch; but was preying on customers' racial and ethnic sensitivities in the bizarre belief this would increase sales.

Criticism, once confined almost exclusively to politics, the arts and sports, is expanding to consumer matters, sometimes even including what used to be called the "big three of the kept press:" the food, real estate and travel sections. A group of consumer reporters recently pondered the question of honesty of newspaper restaurant reviews at the recent Northwestern University conference on con—sumer journalism. Their conclusion: if the majority of reviews are not yet anything more than *quid—pro—quos* for advertising, there is still a remarkable upsurge of candor about such matters as food quality, service and cleanliness. Mike Royko of the Chicago *Daily News* has even tackled the beer industry, claiming domestic beer tastes "as if the secret brewing process involved running it through a horse."

The distance that has been traveled can be measured in the remarkable change of attitude toward the work of Ralph Nader. In the mid—1960s, shortly after the publication of *Unsafe at Any Speed,* the Bell McClure Syndicate set out to sell serial rights to newspapers. Reportedly, it received about 800 refusals before a single taker could be found, the Troy (Ohio) *Daily News,* which was hit with an ad—vertising boycott by local auto dealers after running the

281

first installment. As former editor Tom Pew recalls, "You can't sell autos unless you advertise, and all the dealers returned to the paper within several weeks."

And therein may lie an important clue to why consumer-oriented journalism has improved to the extent it has. More and more publishers, ever conscious of the bottom line, are realizing that such journalism can do wonders for reader credibility. The Minneapolis *Star* discovered this in 1971 after printing a series on the quality of ground beef sold in the Twin Cities area. The meat fared so poorly that for a while it was almost impossible to sell a hamburger in Minneapolis; in a readership survey, the *Star* found the series was its best–read and recalled story.

But while the outlook for consumer journalism is unquestionably bright in many respects, for most papers and stations, it is still "business as usual." Some examples:

—A Pennsylvania publisher read the riot act to his staff after an innocuous Federal Trade Commission press release on how to buy a new car found its way into his paper. The story said nothing more ferocious than that the consumer should negotiate hard, but the publisher hit the roof. "Businessmen are not our natural enemies," he stormed in a memo to his editor. The message got across effectively. The editor says he now thinks twice before he runs any story dealing with consumer matters—"once about whether the story *should* be run, and once about the business office."

—Another Pennsylvania publisher ordered that no local businesses were to be named in his paper's action line column, although it could continue to cite the *governmental* agencies found falling down on the job.

282

—One of the nations's most respected editors recently said in private that he can't speak about consumer journalism because his competitor's ad salesman might use the occasion to convince prospective clients that his paper doesn't offer "the right advertising climate."

(I regret that personal confidences prevent me from naming the above—mentioned editors and publishers.)

—The International Telephone and Telegraph Company, which certainly enjoys no immunity from press criticism about its involvement in the political process, has nevertheless been able to get dozens of gushingly favorable stories about its huge Palm Coast land development in Florida by offering little more than travel and booze to junket—hungry editors and reporters. The corporation's advertising glosses over some potentially ably good job of

covering national consumer news, and there is something to this claim. But at the local level there is often a distinct

reluctance to follow up national stories that have local relevance (particularly if that relevance involves local merchants). When Rep. Wright Patman reported two years ago that a special survey of 300 of the nation's largest banks showed that 80 per cent of them were using a highly questionable, if not illegal, method of calculating interest charges on consumer loans, the story appeared in hundreds of papers, according to Patman's office. But a Patman assistant said later that only two papers did local follow-ups naming specific banks.

More often than not, the press shies away from reporting this sort of dubious marketplace practice that falls technically within the prescribed limits of the law. In each of the past four years, the American Press Institute has asked approximately 100 editors and reporters to select and submit examples of their toughest consumer reporting. Almost all the stories submitted have dealt with the dance studios that bilk lonely old people or other fly—by—night operations. While the patently illegal shennigans of the fly—by—nights are very much a part of consumer journalism, and should be covered by every news organization, so should the comparably pernicious practices that, while legal, are equally unethical. A good example is the "pink light tactic"—displaying meat to unfair advantage under red or pink lights—commonly employed by supermarkets and butchers throughout the country. At last count, only a handful of states and cities defined the practice as deceptive and illegal.

While newspapers rarely cover this sort of deception, much to the detriment of the consumer, extraordinary things can happen when they do. A few years ago, the Miami *Herald* reported that most Florida retailers had adopted the previous balance method of accounting on their charge accounts which squeezed out higher finance charges from their customers). No less than half a dozen class–action suits were instituted against retailers by *Herald* readers. Such is the power of publicity.

More papers might also consider evaluating products and services. There are obvious limitations to what a news organization can take upon itself to do, but there are editors already convinced that it is a logical extension of their work to size up products and services their readers are likely to use. At least three papers, the St. Petersburg *Times,* the Lakeland (Florida) *Ledger* and the Louisville *Times,* now regularly publish reports on the validity of ad claims. The Minneapolis *Star* has done comparative evaluations of funeral services, gasolines, hamburgers, savings accounts and even martinis.

Yet another general failure of the press is its unwillingness to encourage greater consumer access. Where is the paper that regularly encourages and runs letters about food

285

matters (and not just generalized complaints about high costs)? There may be as many as a dozen or two that do, but the rest do not. Where are the real estate sections that offer meaningful letters to the editor?

Perhaps the most notable shortcoming in consumer reporting is the failure of so many editors and news directors to realize that consumer journalism is not just another sub-category of news like, say, high school sports or fashions. Most broadly considered, it is an all pervading attitude towards news itself, and as such could permeate every section of the paper and virtually every article. Publishers like Nelson Poynter of the St. Petersburg papers, the Binghams in Louisville and the Cowles in Minneapolis have had this perspective for a long time and have consistently delivered good, often outstanding, consumer products to their readers. In the words of Rance Crain, president of the company that publishes *Advertising Age*: "It's a fiction that advertisers want nice, safe editorial fare that offends no one. They want papers with impact, that readers can react to."

For all the signs of positive change, the weight of the evidence unfortunately suggests it will be a while before the news media generally will be willing to break the inhibitions of the past, and finally lay to rest the ghost of Upton Sinclair.

19

THE SUPERFICIALITY OF SOCIAL SCIENCE REPORTING

James E. Grunig

Social sciences, which deal with everyday and familiar behavior of human beings, are an easy target, in and out of the press. It is easy to poke fun at the seemingly obvious conclusions drawn by a psychologist, sociologist, or econo—mist. By the same token, it is often easier to poke fun in print rather than to attempt a serious analytical piece.

Plate tectonics and DNA are more technical and unfami—liar concepts than are the mores of the American family or the sociological implications of welfare payments; thus they are less subject to distortion by "common sense" analysis. By and large—with some notable exceptions—social science research receives either poor or distorted coverage in newspapers. A typical and inevitable editorial comment about a newly reported piece of social science research is, "Isn't this what every taxi driver knows, only written in complicated language?"

An important reason for the generally low quality of social science reporting, as I perceive it, is that most newspaper science writers are more familiar with the natural sciences than with the social sciences and therefore share many of the same biases as natural scientists. I've heard both science writers and natural scientists describe the social sciences as pseudo—sciences, soft sciences, soft-work, and so on. Both groups fail to recognize some of the important differences, the most important being that human behavior is more variable than the behavior of atoms, cells, or even guinea pigs. It is no surprise that social scientists have a harder time constructing rigorous theories.

Studies have indicated that newspapers have little interest in social science reporting. Surveys conducted in 1951, 1958, and 1965 by the National Association of Science Writers and New York University (as reported in Hillier Krieghbaum's *Science and the Mass Media*) showed that only 12, 2.9, and 15.7 percent, respectively, of a sample of editors said their newspapers had a special interest in the social sciences. In contrast, about 80 percent of the editors surveyed in each year said their papers had a special interest in medicine and public health, and except in 1951, satellites and outer space.

Krieghbaum also reported results of several studies which indicate that few writers took any social science courses in college, although most did take at least some natural science courses. In contrast, political and foreign reporters took about *half* of their college coursework in the social sciences.

Assuming its inclusion as a social science, economics is perhaps the most accurately and thoroughly covered by newspapers. Bernard Nossiter of the *Washington Post* pointed out at a meeting of the American Economic Association in 1971 that ''the general reader can now find reasonably lucid

288

and not unworthy accounts of economic affairs in at least five daily newspapers published in Boston, New York, Washington, and Los Angeles. For those elsewhere, our one national daily, the *Wall Street Journal,* is far from an adequate substitute." Although Nossiter intended to report progress in economic reporting, his statement would also indicate that he thinks little of the economic reporting done by papers other than those six.

However, most economic reporting is *not* science writing. It is the reporting of economic events, statistics, and predictions. Seldom are the theories underlying those phenomena explained or even reported. Even less often is original economic research ever reported. For example, at the 1971 AEA meeting, the journalists spent more time discussing the difficulty of getting truthful information from government economists than they did reporting the science of economics.

Next to economics, psychology probably gets the most newspaper coverage of the social sciences. But only the mental health and clinical aspects of psychology get much attention. Political science and sociology make the media from time to time, particularly during the annual meetings of the American Political Science Association and the American Sociological Association. But these sciences generally get coverage only when research findings relate to such "newsworthy" events as elections, polls, riots, and commissions on violence, television, and pornography.

Newspapers also tend to report social science when they think it will make an interesting feature or curiosity piece. In these instances, writers or editors seize upon and toy with social science research which confirms their intuitive reasoning or which they think will amuse their readers.

With good reason, social scientists believe such reporting belittles their work.

Examples of this side of social science reporting—the belittling variety—come from work that students have done in my science writing class at the University of Maryland. For example, one student wrote a story about a psychologist's research on the effect physical attractiveness has on the way people evaluate other people. In one experiment, the researchers found that a mock jury gave an attractive female a lighter sentence if the crime was a burglary, but a heavier sentence if she had been accused of using her beauty to swindle a man. The student's story was straightforward and accurate. It began:

The physical attractiveness of a criminal defendent may influence the judgments of juries, according to social psychologist Harold Sigall of the University of Maryland.

Dr. Sigall recently completed an experiment which indicates that a defendent's attractiveness, under our present court system, can be both an advantage and disadvantage. "How beauty can affect the sentencing of an individual," Sigall says, "is determined by the nature of the crime."

The student's story was released through the university's news bureau after some rewriting and was subsequently picked up by wire services and by papers throughout the country. Some of the more accurate headlines read, "Beauty can Help Woman in Court, Study Shows" and "Good Looks Given Edge in Court." But others read, "Sexy Crooks Reward," and "If You're a Woman, Look Attractive."

290

One of the worst treatments of the story was in the *Washington Star–News*, where the writer used much of the university press release but then added to the story by interviewing several judges and prosecutors to ask if the findings were true. As most social scientists know, a sample of one (or three in this case) can never reveal anything and seldom can the subject of an experiment confirm the findings.

Newsworthy and curiosity stories may fit the conventional news judgments of most newspaper editors, but from a scientific standpoint these stories are generally based on the least useful and least typical kinds of social science research. Social science research, like any scientific research, is most valuable if it contributes to theory. Yet most social science reporting is based on what I would call empirical generalizations. In other words, the results are interesting and perhaps of practical use in the type of situation from which the data were collected, but the results contribute little to an abstract and powerful theory that explains and predicts many situations.

Social science is not suffused with abstract theory, and thus its research often appears unrelated and faddish. But good theory is being developed, and, if members of the public are to understand the relevance of social science to their lives, they will have to be helped to better understanding of these theories. Members of the public could, for example, understand the effect of television on their lives better if they understood social systems theory, could understand the national debt better if they understood the nature of an internal debt, and could understand a child's learning process better if they understood operant conditioning.

My own communications research shows that theory can be communicated to people if its implications are relevant

291

to their life situation. For example, people don't care about inflation when there is none, or about learning theories when they have no children.

I have also found that people can better understand the theories if the writer compares the abstract concepts to concepts familiar to the reader. Analogies and parables (stories of people experiencing the theory's implications) work particularly well. For example, I have compared the national debt to a husband loaning money to his wife. I have compared tax breaks to welfare payments. Agricultural and business magazines have used parables for years, for example when they write about a farmer who has adopted a new technology or a businessman who has run a successful business.

Many editors would object that this type of social science reporting might help some people to understand social science and thus would be good for social scientists, but it would be bad for newspaper circulation in that few readers would be interested. Perhaps that is why Nossiter could name only six papers (all with sophisticated audiences) who do credible economic writing. Perhaps these editors are correct, but I believe newspapers have the obligation to report information that is relevant to the lives of their readers, even if they must use extra effort to get people to read it.

Communication research shows that people will seek information relevant to their life situations. Since social science deals with human behavior, it should always be relevant to people's lives. To bridge the gap between theory and everyday life, however, requires a skillful writer who can explain the relevance of a theory without destroying its meaning.

292

INDEX

294

295